OPTIMIZING TALENT WORKBOOK

Building an Unbeatable Talent Brand

What people are saying
about Optimizing Talent

"The authors provide an easy-to-read, step-by-step approach to building talent. Most importantly, they have provided the data and the analytics that prove the steps work."

— NAZNEEN RAZI, SVP and Chief Human Resources Officer, Health Care Services Corporation

"Good organizations spend a lot of time and effort trying to 'manage talent,' often with disappointing results. The authors' excellent framework and examples will help you understand what organizations are doing wrong, and more importantly what you need to do to optimize talent and improve your organization's performance. This is a much-needed book!"

— JEAN-FRANCOIS MANZONI, PhD, Professor, IMD School of Business

"This is a must-read for leaders who want to get the most out of their talent equations and who believe their workforce is critical to their own success. Use it to assess what you are doing today and follow the advice to get the most out of your team."

— MARK HUTCHINSON, Vice President, General Electric Real Estate, GE International

"The Talent Optimization Framework™ is a proven tool to help you assess where you are relative to talent and build a clear strategy to achieve lasting results."

— LOUIS CARTER, Founder and CEO, Best Practice Institute

OPTIMIZING TALENT
WORKBOOK

Building an Unbeatable Talent Brand

LINDA D. SHARKEY PhD
SARAH McARTHUR

IAP

INFORMATION AGE PUBLISHING, INC.
Charlotte, NC • www.infoagepub.com

Library of Congress Cataloging-in-Publication Data

A CIP record for this book is available from the Library of Congress
http://www.loc.gov

ISBN: 978-1-62396-709-3 (Paperback)
       978-1-62396-710-9 (ebook)

Printed in the United States of America

Dedication

*To my husband Tom for all his love and support and to my
parents who would have been so proud of this accomplishment.*
— LINDA D. SHARKEY PhD

*Dedicated to Homer, from whom I learned and with
whom I've found that anything is possible!*
— SARAH McARTHUR

Contents

Preface

*D*ear Readers,

If you have read *Optimizing Talent: What Every Leader and Manager Needs to Know to Build the Ultimate Workforce*, this workbook will help you put the ideas and concepts into action. If you haven't, we suggest you get a copy, take the survey (www.lindasharkey.com), and then use this workbook to set a concrete plan for action. We have specifically written the workbook to help you walk through each of the necessary steps for success as outlined in the *Optimizing Talent* book.

As you begin, we hope you'll not be put off by the fact that the journey to the top quartile of talent-rich organizations may take some time and will definitely require effort. However, we believe it is a journey worth taking, especially as we've made it easier to make. The Optimizing Talent Model™ is designed to assist you in fluidly raising the bar on your talent practices no matter where you are currently in the process. If you are just starting, or are well on your way, this approach will be very useful to you. Use the workbook yearly to reflect on your progress, reassess where you stand, and plan for the strategy going forward. This is a strategic planning template for you, your team, your business leaders, and your organization at large to strengthen your talent brand and thus reap the benefits of attracting and retaining the best talent.

We have seen organizations use the Talent Optimization Framework™ and approach to build consistent global practices as they move from being multinational organizations to being truly global enterprises. This workbook provides the framework for all parts of your organization to use as they spread globally. It creates a common language of how to think about talent globally and how to work with new partners and companies that you may be acquiring or with whom you may be involved in a partnership or joint venture. The approach outlined here allows all of your organizational entities to develop their talent strategy based upon their own unique needs and where they are on their particular journey. In a global and emerging market arena, a "one-size-fits-all" talent approach will likely not drive success. Using a model that allows for local nuances and is adaptable and flexible enough for diverse circumstances strengthens the organization's talent capability, builds alliances, and creates solid global relationships.

A common framework will enable your organization to move talent effectively around the globe and build strong talent pools no matter where you are doing business. This common framework is the essential glue for any company, small or large, public or private or not-for-profit, to succeed and compete for the best talent in the world and, most importantly, to retain that talent. This model can also be used as a framework for understanding the talent practices of companies that you may be considering acquiring. Take a look and you'll get a firsthand view of the practices in place, a snapshot of the commonalities and differences in the global talent arena, and where these commonalities and differences may create conflict or synergy.

We have laid out a step-by-step strategic implementation approach for developing and retaining the best talent wherever you do business. We hope you enjoy the book and look forward to hearing from you about your progress!

LINDA D. SHARKEY PhD
Southport, NC

SARAH MCARTHUR
San Diego, CA

About the Authors

LINDA D. SHARKEY PhD is an internationally recognized expert in the field of global leadership development and culture transformation. Her specific area of focus is using science and data to underpin her work and assure alignment to business results and outcomes. Linda is a noted international keynote speaker and executive coach. She is a recognized author on leadership and talent and most recently co-authored the award winning book *Winning with Transglobal Leadership: How to Develop and Retain Top Global Talent*. Prior to her current consulting practice, she was Chief Talent Officer for Hewlett Packard and held numerous executive human resources positions at GE. Her leadership work at GE was named a "best practice" by former GE CEO Jack Welsh. Currently, Dr. Sharkey is a founding member of the Marshall Goldsmith Group a preeminent executive coaching firm, and partner at Achieveblue a top-tier leadership development consulting firm. She received her Ph.D. with honors from Benedictine University in Lisle, Illinois.

SARAH MCARTHUR is founder of *sdedit, a writing and editing firm based in San Diego, California. With two decades of experience in the publishing field, Sarah has worked with such influential clients as Marshall Goldsmith and Anthony Robbins. She has played significant roles in the best-sellers *What Got You Here Won't Get You There* and *Mojo: Hot to Get It, How to Keep It, and How to Get It Back If You Lose It*. Sarah is author and co-editor of the classic title *Coaching for Leadership: Writings on Leadership from the World's Greatest Coaches* with Marshall Goldsmith and Laurence S. Lyons and *The AMA Handbook of Leadership* with Marshall Goldsmith and John Baldoni. This book received the Top 10 Business, Management, and Labour Title Award of 2010 from Choice. As managing and developmental editor of numerous highly successful business and leadership titles, Sarah is a highly sought-after freelance editor and writing coach. She has held editorial and management positions at The San Diego Reader, Harcourt Brace & Company, and The Anthony Robbins Companies. She is former editor of *Business Coaching Worldwide*, and was graduated from the University of Oregon with degrees in English and Environmental Studies.

Acknowledgements

We would like to acknowledge all of the great thinkers who contributed to this book as well as the companies and leaders we have worked with who have applied these concepts to great success. Special thanks to publisher George Johnson and his team. We would also like to thank Kathy Hyatt Stewart our exceptional copyeditor who has an eye for detail and a nose for references, and Nick Isabella, our graphic designer, who has an extraordinary knack for making business books pleasing to the eye and an easy, professional attitude. They both contributed greatly to making this book a success. Finally, thanks to our family and friends whose support and encouragement never seem to wane.

CHAPTER ONE

GETTING STARTED

by Linda D. Sharkey PhD.

Have you ever read an inspiring business book and when you finished, asked yourself, "Well, that was great, now what do I do?" Similar questions might have come to mind, like, "How do I get started implementing the ideas presented? What are the practical steps I can take to move these ideas and concepts forward? How do I go about getting buy-in from my leadership team?" Most of us have been in your situation. That's why we have decided to help the many readers of *Optimizing Talent: What Every Leader and Manager Needs to Know to Sustain the Ultimate Workforce* (Sharkey and Eccher, 2010) by providing the next step. In this workbook, you'll find hands-on advice about HOW to implement the ideas put forth in *Optimizing Talent* and make your organization a great talent powerhouse!

Imagine you have a magic wand and you know immediately how to apply these techniques to your organization. Imagine your colleagues saying to you, "WOW! Where did you get all these great insights?" Imagine your leadership team and CEO saying, "You have brought real talent innovation to the table. It is practical, actionable, and can produce real business results." How would you feel? Hopefully you would feel on top of the world. That is how we want you to feel, and it is the purpose of the *Optimizing Talent Workbook*.

The *Optimizing Talent Workbook* is designed to give you a personal competitive advantage in the talent and workforce planning space. If you follow and apply these tools and techniques, you will be ensured of creating a talent brand for your company that will "WOW" the external marketplace, attract top potential employees, and bring a WOW to the lips of your existing employee base. You my think this is impossible. We don't. Take a look at the workbook, try the ideas, and see for yourself.

My coauthor, Paul Eccher, and I are humbled by the many great comments and feedback we receive about *Optimizing Talent*. Some teams told us that they used our book as the basis of a book review and for human resources discussion and study groups. Other teams reported that they summarized it and made their own work plans from it.

These responses inspired us to think of a next logical step for the book, and after much deliberation and conversation, we decided to put together a comprehensive workbook. Each chapter of the workbook is written by either me or a key expert in each quadrant of the Optimizing Talent Framework. Each expert has unique experience implementing these talent approaches in such significant companies as IBM, Novartis, Apple, General Electric (GE), Hewlett-Packard (HP), and Avaya, to name but a few. We call these stellar contributors to the *Optimizing Talent Workbook* the "pracademics" in the field, i.e., those who have the scholarly background and research to support their suggestions and techniques, and also have implemented these techniques to great success in some of the world's most successful companies.

Using the Optimizing Talent Workbook, *you will learn step-by-step how to:*

- Analyze your current situation;

- Follow a guided process for determining how to address your current situation;

- Implement tools and techniques to move your talent processes forward;

- Create specific actions to close the gaps;

- Define how you will measure progress;

- Tell a compelling story of progress that even your CEO can't resist.

How to Use This Workbook

The very first step in getting started is to discover where you stand today relative to the Optimizing Talent Framework. (See the model and its definitions in Figure 1.1.)

FIG 1.1: THE TALENT OPTIMIZATION FRAMEWORK™

Please log into our website (www.lindasharkey.com) and take the Talent Optimization Framework Survey™. A report will be generated that can help you pinpoint both your strengths and the areas that need improvement. Next, have your team take the survey and discuss the results with them. It is recommended that you involve more people in the survey than just yourself. That way you can get a more robust perspective of what is going on relative to your talent practices. Completing the survey will give you a baseline of where you are today. Using this diagnostic will give you a jumping-off point and a baseline measurement that will be extremely helpful in tracking your progress and revealing tangible results.

Once you have reviewed the results of the survey, you should narrow the components that you believe are in most need of improvement. That said, you should also go through each section to test all the components to see if you are on target or could elevate the performance of a particular component even more.

Each section of this workbook follows the Talent Optimization Framework™. There are exercises in each section that help you diagnose what you are currently doing. Ideas for improvement are offered. Last but not least, you can log into our chat line at www.lindasharkey.com, and ask the experts and authors of each chapter for some advice and feedback. This is a great way to test your ideas before you begin your implementation process.

What's New About This Workbook?

Rather than just recapping the *Optimizing Talent* book, we've added some new content on topics we've seen emerging since the book was published and a few other perks you'll only find here. For instance, we've included a chapter about talent branding, and the performance management chapter is written from the angle of neuroscience, which we know you will find fascinating. In addition to case studies throughout the book, Chapter Eleven includes three specific cases where talent systems have been implemented with study questions to help further your understanding of implementation success and pitfalls.

Talent Branding

In our many speaking and consulting engagements about talent processes, we consistently hear about "employer branding." In fact, much is written about employer branding, which we believe puts a marketing spin on trying to attract employees. This isn't a bad thing, but if the marketing spin does not match the reality of the company when a new employee joins it, then you have done yourself and your organization a great disservice. Word will spread that the reality of your organization does not match the marketing. Social media will ensure this!

Once this mismatch between what you say publicly about your organization and what your organization actually does internally gets out, your reputation will be hard to recover. With social media and websites like www.glassdoor.com, it can take only minutes for your reputation to be tarnished and it can take a very long time to get it back.

In addition, as you'll see in our results section, if you create a strong internal brand, you will create a strong external brand. What your employees say about you creates the marketplace reality for your company and, as such, it creates a strong employer brand. The two go hand in hand.

Companies that have the best internal talent management have strong market brands and are talent magnets. Talent want to work in these organizations, which are in turn widely recognized with leadership and talent awards, such as Fortune's "Best Place for Leaders."

We know of a company that spent a great deal of time recruiting and messaging to potential candidates. It had a beautiful website and great social media campaigns with very slick material. When candidates interviewed, company representatives were on their best behavior. However, once the candidate was hired, the picture changed. Leaders were abusive. Employees were thrown into environments to sink or swim with little or no support. The organizational culture did not reflect a focus on talent or career development as the website had indicated. Employees were criticized for minor mistakes. And, word got out. Retention became difficult. Existing employees told their networks not to work for the organization. The retention and recruiting nightmare was in full cycle. And this is an incredibly difficult cycle to break!

Throughout the *Optimizing Talent Workbook*, we will provide you with practical tips and methods for making your internal brand congruent with your employer brand. We'll focus on the subject of talent branding in Chapter Two. Talent branding is a new term that combines talent management practices and employer branding. Chapter Two will provide you with a model of what to think about to ensure there is alignment between what you say about your organization and what your organization actually does. This insightful chapter, written by Sarah McArthur, will provide you with an indispensable perspective on how to build a strong and lasting talent brand for your organization. The chapter provides the foundation for what you need to do and think about with regards to talent branding, and if you follow the steps outlined in this chapter, you will be sure to shine in the marketplace.

Neuroscience

Performance management is a hot button for many companies. Most managers and employees don't like the "forced-ranking" system. Feedback is a chore, because it is viewed as a negative exercise focusing on someone's personal deficiencies. Studies have shown, as discussed in Chapter Six, that today's approaches to performance management have the opposite effect of their proposed intention. They don't improve performance as they are currently constructed.

Organizations spend lots of time and money trying to perfect systems that just about everyone hates. From neuroscientific research, we have learned how to create performance management systems that not only improve performance, but also create the intended impact of improvement that the system was designed to achieve. This chapter will help you pinpoint the areas that block your organization from having a world-class feedback and coaching system that yields true performance improvement.

Recently, we worked with a company to help reframe their performance management system. The CEO wanted it abolished completely, the lawyers and human resources wanted to keep it for compliance and compensation reasons, and the employees and managers hated it. The managers wanted to coach employees to greater heights of achievement and were willing to commit the time and energy to do so – how is this possible given this misalignment? If this story sounds familiar to you, then delve into the chapter and rethink your system using the researched concepts we provide and methods that have been scientifically proven to energize people, not demotivate them!

Phil Dixon, the chapter's author, eloquently points out how neuroscience has proven that performance management systems as currently constructed have the net opposite effect from what is intended. Feedback focused on flaws cause the receiver to retreat to a defensive mode as opposed to attempt to get better.

Current systems are designed to document poor performance of the less than 10% of employees who are not up to par. This seems like a lot of effort for a small population, and it misses the bulk of employees who are wired to do a good job and want to improve. Phil's chapter about performance management will help you rethink your current performance management system and create one that will "pop" in the eyes of all users.

Case Studies

Throughout the *Optimizing Talent Workbook*, there are case studies that will help you see how other organizations have done what is suggested in each chapter. Chapter Ten, by Eve Emerson, includes two specific case studies where talent systems have been implemented – one in a large technology company, another in a mid-sized company, and the third in a small start-up environment. Each of the case studies includes study questions that will help you to analyze each situation and provide invaluable insight into what was done well and what could have been done more successfully or differently.

These case studies are teaching tools for leadership teams that are interested in having a world-class organization, whether the organization is Zappos.com, IBM, or a Rodan and Fields. If you do your analysis and want to know what happened in one of the cases, send your analysis to our chat line and we will provide you with feedback on your approach.

Chat Opportunities with the Experts

Each chapter and its exercises are written by an expert in that area. We've included a short bio of each contributor at the end of this workbook. Once you have gone through each section of the workbook, you can contact the experts for some quick guidance on your plan using our chat line. This will give you the assurance that you are going in the right direction and it can give you a sounding board for tough questions. Who does not want some expert advice? This is a unique opportunity to talk to Dan Martin about assessment and alignment, to Lynda Keating about culture transformation, to Frank Wagner about critical development approaches and how to leverage coaching for real change results, to Liza Sichon about how to transform human resources with all its challenges, and to me about all facets of the Talent Optimization Framework™ and workforce planning.

Road Map to Success

Finally, in Chapter Eleven, you will find a road map to success upon which you can formulate your strategy and plan, track your results, and highlight your successes and next steps. In this chapter, we have provided all of the checklists from each chapter. From them, you will see how to measure your progress and what to do to continue the talent journey. This road map will provide you with the hard evidence you need to see how you can transform the talent focus in your organization and how you can build the optimal workforce that everyone dreams of.

Who Should Use This Workbook?

This workbook is designed for anyone who knows that talent is the one true competitive advantage. Without great talent and a supportive culture led by constructive leaders, growth is elusive. Energy is wasted on nonproductive activities. Time at the workplace becomes a chore rather than fun. Any sense of achievement is lost.

We've all experienced great joy in some workplaces and been in the doldrums in others. If you believe that people make the difference in creating cultures of high performance and you have a personal stake in making your workplace a powerhouse for talent and marketplace success, then work through our chapters. Build a plan and follow it. You will be successful and you will leave a legacy of amazing talent and a great organization. Whether you are just beginning your journey or well along the way, it is time to get started optimizing your talent!

CHAPTER TWO

TALENT BRANDING

by Sarah McArthur

With the onset of the knowledge worker – people who know more about what they are doing than their bosses do – there are a couple of challenges. The first is that it's hard to tell people what to do and how to do it when they know more than you do. Second, these knowledge workers are often and increasingly less "full-time, lifelong" employees and more "temporary individual contractors." Even if not termed "part-time," these associates should be regarded as such. This is a workforce with the option of mobility. The challenge we'll focus on in this chapter is just this – they can leave, you want them to stay, how do you get what you want?

As Peter Drucker wrote, "Altogether, an increasing number of people who are full-time employees have to be managed as if they were volunteers. They are paid, to be sure. But knowledge workers have mobility. They can leave. They own their "means of production," which is their knowledge." (Drucker, 2001) The Great Recession of the last decade put a damper on some of this mobility for a time, but as we rebound from that economic decline, more and more opportunities are presenting themselves for the knowledge workforce.

Add to the fact that your talent probably doesn't have to stay at your company to be employed the advent of new technology and rapid-fire growth of social media platforms like Twitter, Facebook, LinkedIn, Google+, and jobsites like Glassdoor.com, US.jobs, Monster.com, CareerBuilder.com, and TweetMyJobs.com, and you have the recipe for disaster if your employer brand does not match up to what it is really like to work at your organization. With the stroke of a few keys, your organization's reputation can be altered, damaged, even ruined as one disgruntled employee spreads her message of discontent with the organization to her hundreds of friends, family, and co-workers, who spread it to their thousands of friends, who spread these seemingly insignificant 140 characters across the globe in just a few minutes on Twitter. It is amazing that something so brief and (possibly) thoughtless can be so devastating so quickly.

As another example, take the employment site Glassdoor.com. This site makes accessible the factors that shape an organization's reputation, such as Facebook, revealing insider information about the hiring processes and work environments of companies. It's an extremely handy tool for job seekers; however, it can be a disaster for organizations whose employer brand does not match up to its talent brand.

While the concept and practice of employer branding have been around for a while, talent branding is a relatively new notion. For our purposes here, we define *talent branding* as the connection between your internal brand (that promoted by your talent from the inside to the outside) and your employer brand. Many leaders talk about their organization's "employer brand" and view marketing the company to potential employees as just that: a marketing campaign. However, if you want to attract and retain the best employees, you have to have both a strong employer brand and a strong talent brand. Even more importantly, these two have to be in alignment. That's because of the advent of social media platforms that link your employees to each other and to workers around the world through methods that are, to a large extent, out of your hands. In a way, it's a good thing, because it keeps the organization "honest," Preventing it from marketing itself as one thing, but in reality being another.

All right, so the case is made that as an organization leader, you want to attract and retain the best employees, i.e., you want to hire and keep knowledge workers. How do you do this? You go beyond employer branding (or external marketing) to connect and align your internal and external brands. You enter the world of talent branding, where you tap your greatest resource: your employees. Your knowledge workers are the best sellers of the organization to other potential employees. They build the company reputation. They recommend the organization as a great place to work to jobsites, family, friends, and followers…or not. How you go about creating your talent brand can be relatively simple.

First, let's assess where your organization is now, the challenges you face with your internal brand. Then, let's take a look at what the benefits would be to the organization of having a great talent brand, where you want to be.

Exercise 2.1: Talent Brand Assessment

1. What do you believe your internal brand is now?

_____

_____

_____

2. What is your employer brand? What brand do you market?

_____

_____

_____

3. *What are people saying about what it is like to work at your organization on jobsites, employee blog sites, and social media platforms, such as Twitter, Facebook, and LinkedIn?*

_____

_____

_____

4. *Is your talent brand in alignment with your employer brand? Why? Why not?*

_____

_____

_____

5. *Is your talent brand in alignment with your internal brand? Why? Why not?*

_____

_____

_____

6. *Does your organization's culture build careers or does it treat/view people as expendable?*

_____

_____

_____

6. *What challenges is the organization/are you facing with regards to developing a strong, sustainable talent brand?*

_____

_____

_____

Exercise 2.2: Benefits of Talent Branding

What are some of the benefits of having a strong talent brand to your company, to your teams, and to your employees? These are your talent branding targets!

1. _____

2. _____

3. _____

4. _____

Now that you have an idea where your organization is currently and where you'd like it to be, take a look Figure 2.1: The Optimizing Talent Branding Model, which we'll go into in greater depth below. Applying this model, you can steer your organization to an excellent talent brand.

FIG 2.1: THE OPTIMIZING TALENT BRANDING MODEL

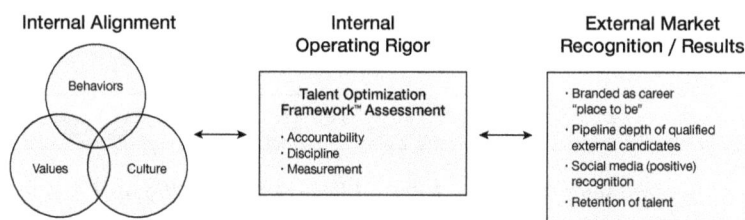

Continuous monitoring to ensure market brand excellence.

Let's begin with the problem that many organizations face: There is a disconnect between the organization's talent and employer brands, and it is significantly affecting morale, attraction, and retention of employees. The solution, as illustrated in Figure 2.1 above, is to create a positive connection between your talent and employer brands. To be great externally, your organization has to be great internally. The challenge is that this connection needs to be built internally, but it is highly doable and incredibly beneficial. Here's how.

Internal Alignment

The first step to realizing a strong talent brand is gauging the alignment (or lack thereof) of your organization's behaviors, culture, and values. For instance, does your organization externally market itself as a great place to advance your career, yet upon coming on board the new hire finds that the culture, behaviors, and values do not reflect this claim? This significant disconnect between employer brand and actuality has the potential to destroy your talent brand. It can ruin your organization's reputation and quickly brand it as a bad place to work.

Internal Operating Rigor

You'll want to test your assumptions about who you are as a company. One great way to do this is with the Talent Optimization Survey™ (www.lindasharkey.com), which will reveal if your organization is putting in significant effort to optimize and develop its talent and in what areas there might be work to do. Also, do some benchmarking. Find out what your employees are saying about your company – what is your reputation? Check out social media sites (Twitter, Facebook, LinkedIn) and the many jobsites, e.g., those mentioned previously, GlassDoor.com, US.jobs, Monster.com, CareerBuilder.com, and TweetMyJobs.com. These social media platforms and jobsites are where your reputation is made.

Reputation is tricky because it's to some extent out of your control, yet it's absolutely critical to your success. According to executive coach Marshall Goldsmith, "Your reputation is a scoreboard kept by others. It's your coworkers, customers, friends (and sometimes strangers who've never met you) grabbing the right to grade your performance—and report their opinions to the rest of the world. Although you can't take total control of your reputation, there's a lot you can do to maintain or improve it," which is just what we're talking about here. (Goldsmith, 2010)

These are just two ways to gain insight into how well your employer brand is aligned with your talent brand. So, find out. What are people saying about your company internally? Externally? Look at your employee engagement scores and people's comments about your organization. These will tell you a lot about what internal employees think about working in the organization.

The next step is to do your action planning. How can you gain alignment between the internal reality and the external brand that you want to be known for? What are the gaps between your employer brand and what it's really like to work in the organization? How can you close these gaps?

When you find yourself in this disconnect, you need to be honest about it. Speak transparently about the misalignments that the organization has and what you are aspiring to have the organization become. Openly share the key actions that you are taking to move the organization towards alignment of its internal and external brands. Honesty and truth telling is the best policy.

External Market Recognition/Results

Key indicators that you are building a great internal brand will be reflected in the external market by your talent brand. If your employees are recommending your organization as a great place to work and develop your career, you are succeeding! Your organization's reputation will grow and you will attract and retain talent as a result.

Chapter Two Checklist

Following is a checklist for you to consider after you have reviewed this chapter and before moving on to the next chapters.

☐ Do you clearly understand your current talent brand?

- Have you checked social media platforms, jobsites, and employee blog sites?

- Have you researched what people are saying to each other about your organization, your leaders, your organization's career development opportunities?

- Have you reviewed your employee surveys?

☐ What is your employee brand?

- What are you promising new hires?

- What is your employee development plan?

- Are your organization's culture, behaviors, and values aligned? Are these reflected in your employee brand?

☐ What methods/tools do you have in place or could you put in place to measure and improve employee engagement/satisfaction?

- Do you have an employee satisfaction survey?

- Are your leaders coaches/mentors to your employees?

If you are confident in your answers that you have what you need to move forward with your talent branding initiative, then you are ready to move on to the next chapter.

Summary

A critical component of being a successful organization today is attracting and retaining great talent. Is your organization regarded as a great place to work by your employees? Does your organization have a reputation as a great place to build a career, to work, grow, learn, and develop? As we've seen throughout this chapter, your organization's talent brand will either attract great talent or cause them to avoid your company altogether. What would your employees say your brand is? Does your marketplace branding reflect what actually happens when a new employee arrives on the job? And, finally do your market (employer brand) and your talent (internal brand) align? If not, take the steps outlined above and apply the Optimizing Talent Branding Model to build alignment and achieve a phenomenal talent brand.

Finally, implementing the information in the subsequent *Optimizing Talent Workbook* chapters is imperative as you focus on building congruence between your external and internal brands. The good news is that the natural consequence of applying these learnings to your organization is talent optimization and a good reputation. The Optimizing Talent method is the best way we have found for establishing a strong internal brand. So take to heart Linda Sharkey's discussion of the talent brand proposition to strategic alignment in Chapter Four, and the critical relationship of leadership and culture to talent branding as discussed in Chapter Seven by Frank Wagner. You'll find that the information in each chapter of this book can be incredibly useful as you align your employer and internal brands to create a strong talent brand.

CHAPTER THREE

LEADERSHIP AND CULTURE

by Lynda Keating

*W*hat Comes First?

As you experience your organization on a day-to-day basis, "What comes first?" often becomes the classic chicken-or-egg question. Does the culture of the organization drive leadership behaviors or do the behaviors of the leadership team drive culture? Edgar H. Schein in his book *Organizational Culture and Leadership* discusses the impact of leaders or "founders" on the development of organizational culture in an organization's early stages; he discusses how the culture molds leaders who grow up in the organization until they consciously choose to change it. (Schein, 2004)

How do the culture and/or the leadership behaviors of your organization impact your ability to attract, develop, and retain top talent for today and tomorrow? In this chapter, we are going to explore together ways that will allow you to assess and leverage the impact and viability of both the talent and the overall engagement of the organization. Of course your culture and leadership style, while having a direct effect on your engagement, also affect how you are viewed in the marketplace from a talent perspective. The culture and leadership behaviors that are in place signal to everyone whether your organization is one that focuses on talent development or one that has a "sink or swim" mentality towards your workforce. Whatever the mentality of your leaders and the culture that has been created, it affects your talent brand both internally and externally. Let's get started.

A Symbiotic Relationship

One thing we know about the relationship between behavior and culture, whether leadership behaviors or employee behaviors, is that if you have chosen to remain with an organization because of opportunity, location, product, or loyalty, you want to fit in and be successful. How do we do that? I have certainly never joined an organization that during orientation provided me with a list of "the do's and don'ts" to being successful or fitting in (wouldn't that be amazing?). I am also sure you have experienced organizations where you felt at home immediately and fit in beautifully and others where you were uncertain, uncomfortable, and ultimately left the organization because you really didn't "fit in." How do we as individuals begin to recognize what is going to make us successful here and whether we can or even want to "fit in"?

In Figure 3.1, we look at how a) we understand the organization, and b) how that understanding impacts our behavior and reinforces the culture of an organization and ultimately the market brand of the company.

FIG 3.1: HOW DO WE EXPERIENCE AND REINFORCE CULTURE?

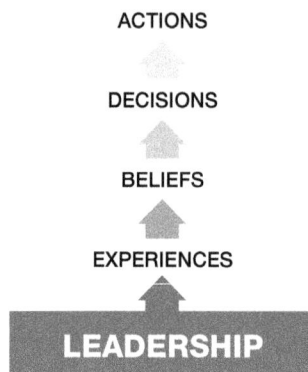

ACTIONS

DECISIONS

BELIEFS

EXPERIENCES

LEADERSHIP

As new joiners to an organization, oftentimes one of the first things that we are provided with is a list of the values of the organization. However, as we experience the organization on a day-to-day basis, we begin to observe behaviors that may not be supportive of those values. For instance, suppose you join an organization which claims that its primary value is innovation. However, every time you approach your new manager with an idea or process that might improve the productivity or output of the team you are told, "That's a nice idea, however that's not how we do things here at New Co." Or, "We tried that in the past and it didn't work," or "Thanks for that, however I think you need to concentrate on learning the ropes before you begin recommending changes." What happens is that you know that innovation is a value, but what you come to believe is that in order to fit in and be successful, you had better figure out how things are done and conform. The belief that develops out of your personal experiences drives your decisions going forward. Are you going to take any new ideas to your boss? No, not if you want to be successful. Those decisions drive behavior that others observe and experience, which reinforces the culture and so on. Ultimately, this is a deciding factor in whether your organization is branded as one that supports talent development or not.

Research as well as common sense tells us that the individual who has the biggest impact on how you experience an organization is your manager or leader. How are you treated? How are others treated? How does he/she speak about their peers or about other parts of the organization? How does he/she share organizational directives? All of these observable behaviors begin to establish our beliefs about what is acceptable, and, more than that, how "successful" people in this organization behave.

You may wonder how this affects talent in an organization. Well, depending on what's in it for individuals, they will very quickly decide if they want to stay with the organization or find a new organization that better suits their personal style and values. If top talent and high potentials consistently decide that this isn't the place for them, it negatively impacts the future of the organization. However, if they decide to stay, they begin to emulate the successful role models that they have, their leaders, and they begin to demonstrate the behaviors that reinforce a less than optimal work environment or culture, which also detracts from the future talent pool.

Breaking the Cycle: A Case Study

As discussed in the last section, behavior and culture drive and reinforce each other in an ongoing cycle. As leaders in an organization, we need to consciously decide to change in order to break the cycle and create new experiences and new beliefs. Ultimately, this will create a new culture that attracts, develops, and retains the kind of talent that guarantees the future of the organization and creates a recognizable positive talent brand both internally and externally.

This is a case study of a global pharmaceutical company and its quest for change. Although performance had been good, the head of one of the key divisions wanted to elevate results by creating and fostering a culture of excellence. The management team felt it was important to ensure that the culture within the division was the best it could be for the employees. The organization was undergoing an acquisition by another global pharmaceutical, and there was a lot of uncertainty within the division regarding job security and sustainability. The team wanted to create an environment of trust and sharing that would retain top talent and ultimately drive overall results.

Process: Engaging her senior leadership team, the head of the division created a profile of what a culture of excellence would ideally look like in order to support sustainable growth, using the Organization Culture Inventory (OCI) to define the OCI Ideal (the OCI was introduced and discussed in Chapter Four of *Optimizing Talent*, Sharkey and Eccher, 2010). The division members were then surveyed as to what behaviors they believed were required to be most successful as they moved into the acquisition, the Current OCI. Concurrently, the leadership team members worked together to identify their impact on overall culture, their own teams, as well as their impact on each other by utilizing the Leadership/Impact™ (L/I) assessment process (introduced in Chapter Six of *Optimizing Talent,* ibid.). The L/I is a 360 tool designed to provide leaders with information regarding their impact on others, as well as the strategies and techniques (behaviors) that account for this impact. As such, the L/I is intended for use in self-development, leadership development, culture change, and organizational development initiatives and programs. (Szumal, 2002)

Figures 3.2 and 3.3 provide examples of the Ideal Culture and the overall Current OCI.

FIG. 3.2: IDEAL CULTURE PROFILE

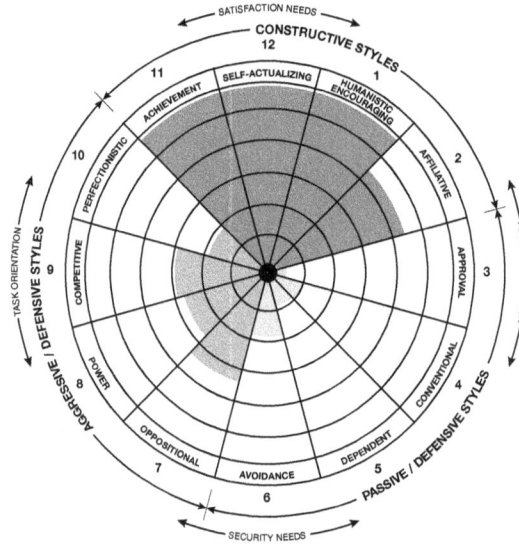

FIG. 3.3: CURRENT LEADERSHIP/IMPACT

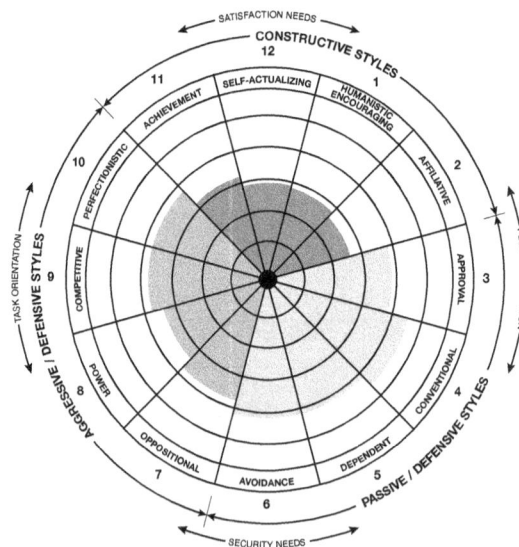

What do these two assessments tell us about this organization?

The Ideal Culture Profile (Figure 3.2) tells us that people should:

- Focus on excellence in everything they do.

- Be creative and innovative in their approach to every task and situation. View change as opportunity.

- Be engaged, respect others' backgrounds and talents and actively seek out the ideas and opinions of others.

- Focus on teamwork and collaboration as a way to share knowledge and experience.

- Concentrate on establishing extraordinary customer focus by being very attentive to both client and colleagues and ensure they are heard.

The Current Leadership/Impact (Figure 3.3) tells us that people feel they are impacted to:

- Focus less on accomplishing objectives given to them by others (Achievement).

- Focus less on providing quality products and services (Self-Actualizing).

- Moderately support others to help them grow and develop with constructive feedback (Humanistic Encouraging).

- Protect their personal interests in all external and internal relationships (Affiliative).

- Make policies and procedures adherence a top priority (Conventional).

- Strongly avoid responsibility and blame by pushing decisions upward or elsewhere (Avoidance).

- Switch priorities to please others (Approval).

- Always get permission before taking action (Dependence).

- Very strongly compete with peers (Competitive).

- Focus on the negative and very aggressively attack the ideas of others (Oppositional).

- Micromanage and fail to trust others (Power).

- Keep on top of things at all times (Perfectionistic).

With the results of the survey, the team was able to clearly identify gaps between the Ideal Cultural profile (OCI) and what was actually happening (L/I). These results were shared across the entire pharmaceutical division and action planning sessions were initiated. This process offered both employees and the management team the opportunity to take personal accountability for specific actions that would help enhance cultural leadership. They worked through an analysis of how leader behavior was leading or lagging towards the attainment of the ideal culture. Each leader committed to individual actions and the teams created shared commitments that he or she felt would lead to a change in culture.

Interim Results

Midway through the change efforts, significant results could be observed, including:

- Both the leadership team and sales force are enhancing communication, sharing successes and best practices regularly. This is helping the entire team.

- Employees are taking increased initiative to bring new ideas forward for consideration. The team is making a concerted effort to enhance listening and build on ideas.

- Emphasis has been placed on individual accountability, and also on fostering a real team environment where people can openly ask for assistance and support.

- The pharmaceutical division was above plan when measuring its success in 2012.

- The team was also recognized by the GM as being leaders in synergistic activities across the company. The pharmaceutical division continues to look for opportunities to leverage the other teams across the larger organization.

Note: This engagement is still underway at the time of this writing, and more concrete results will be available soon.

What Can You Do in Your Organization?

Of course, the best possible course of action would be to utilize the OCI and L/I to measure and establish a clear plan for change as was done in the case study above. However, if that isn't possible in the immediate future, here are a series of exercises that can easily be worked through with your team.

Based on Figure 3.4, the exercises will assist you in assessing the ways in which you can align your leadership behaviors to the strategy of the organization and create a clear plan to stop behaviors that don't support the values of the organization, Keep doing those behaviors that are supportive and start doing things differently that will create a clear plan for renewal.

FIG 3.4: FOUNDATIONS AND BUSINESS DRIVERS

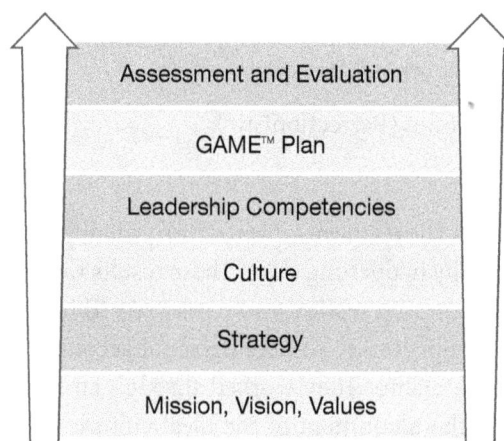

Exercise 3.1: Aligning Your Strategy and Values

This exercise can be done either as an individual exercise or in small groups with a large team debrief, looking at the common themes and where we have different ideas.

1. *Start by recording your mission and vision.*

   _____

   _____

   _____

2. *Record your organizational strategic goals and articulate how each one supports the attainment of the mission and/or vision. One of the most import things that employees like to know and under stand is how their goals and accountabilities support the organizational goals.*

   _____

   _____

   _____

3. *Now record your values and align them to the strategic goals. Please note that they may align to multiple goals.*

   _____

   _____

   _____

4. *Identify any gaps. What do you need to do to close the gaps if you have discovered any?*

   _____

   _____

   _____

Exercise 3.2: Aligning Your Leadership Behaviors

Although this can be done on an individual basis, this exercise works best in small group discussions.

1. *Based on the results from Exercise 3.1, align each of the leadership behaviors to the values of your organization. Remember that they can align to multiple values.*

   _____

   _____

   _____

2. *As a team, record on a flip chart all the behaviors you experience or even demonstrate on a day-to-day basis that support the values of the organization. Keep going until you have descriptors for all of the behaviors.*

_____

_____

_____

3. *Now look at the other side of the coin and record on a separate flip chart all the behaviors that you experience, observe, or demonstrate on a daily basis that are counter to the leadership behaviors as you have described them.*

_____

_____

_____

4. *Discuss how both sets of behaviors impact the way in which employees experience the organization. What might this lead them to believe about what will make them successful and allow them to fit in here?*

_____

_____

_____

Exercise 3.3: Stop, Start, Keep

1. *Identify at least one to three behaviors from Exercise 3.2 that you want to Stop doing and why. How will this improve the experience of your employees and most importantly your top talent?*

_____

_____

_____

2. *Identify one to three behaviors that you feel would be important to Start doing in order to significantly improve the experience of your employees.*

_____

_____

_____

3. *Identify one to three behaviors that you want to Keep doing and why. How are they impacting the experience of your employees currently?*

_____

_____

_____

4. *Prioritize your items using Nominal Group Technique and write GAME™ Plan goals for the top items. They can be Stops, Starts, or Keeps.*

_____

_____

_____

5. *Now integrate these goals into your accountabilities for the year.*

_____

_____

_____

Nominal Group Technique: How To

1. *Provide each voting member with a card.*

2. *Ask them to select their top 3 items in order of descending priority.*
   #1= 3 points;   #2 = 2 points;   and #3 = 1 point.

3. *Record your point scores against each item selected.*

4. *Tally the results and identify the item with the highest score. That is the one you will begin the GAME™ Plan goals with.*

Creating a GAME™ Plan Goal

Goaled Accountability	Metrics	Expectations
Linking back through all three exercises, identify the strategic goal that your behavioral goal will support. Describe exactly what you expect the team to be accountable for in making these behavioral changes.	How will you measure success? • Short-term and long-term retention • Employee engagement scores • 360 results	Specifically describe what "good" looks like. Specifically describe what "outstanding" will look like.

Exercise 3.4: Are You Creating a Culture that Is Supportive of Talent?

As we have been discussing throughout this chapter, to build a supportive culture, leaders must develop a culture and organization where values are clear and behaviors support those values in order to build the kind of culture that you desire (Sharkey and Eccher, 2010).

Individually rate yourself and your organization against the followings statement from 1 (being the lowest) to 10 (being the highest).

Yourself / Organization

_____ _____ *1. Do others know your values and what you stand for?*

_____ _____ *2. Do you operate consistently with your values? How do you know?*

_____ _____ *3. Do you coach your employees to be the best they can be?*

_____ _____ *4. Are you visible when it comes to developing talent?*

_____ _____ *5. Do you participate in development programs?*

_____ _____ *6. Do you seek out talent and help promote careers?*

_____ _____ *7. Do you "walk the talk" and seek feedback on how you are doing?*

_____ _____ *8. Do you work on your own self-development?*

_____ _____ *9. Do you give honest feedback so that people know where they stand?*

_____ _____ *10. Do you actively promote your company leadership brand in the marketplace?*

Chapter Three Checklist

Before moving on to Chapter Four, review the checklist below to ensure that you are creating a culture that is supportive of talent.

- ☐ Ensure you understand and are able to articulate the alignment between what you do (accountabilities/goals) and why you do it (mission/strategies).

- ☐ Verify alignment between the goals, the values, and leadership behaviors.

- ☐ Create a Stop/Start/Keep action plan that drives behaviors that support the values and create the experiences that develop the culture you desire.

- ☐ Embed these actions into leaders' goals and measures.

- ☐ Verify that you are developing a talent-supportive culture.

Summary

Creating a positive culture and having the alignment around the leadership behaviors is the bedrock for any talent system. Being clear is the essential first step in driving change and creating the brand you want. Our research shows that with such a foundation in place and leaders who are willing to look at themselves, a constructive talent strategy will work. In the next chapters, we will explore other ways to gain congruence among your leaders and organization; however, beginning with the exercises in this chapter will make the journey a lot easier. This is because a supportive culture with aligned leader behaviors is the bedrock for success. In fact, *Optimizing Talent* unequivocally demonstrated that supportive culture and leadership behaviors were the single greatest factors in having a successful talent management system.

CHAPTER FOUR

———————————————————————

STRATEGIC ALIGNMENT

by Linda D. Sharkey PhD

Strategy should ensure that everyone in the organization is headed in the same direction for what the organization is trying to achieve. It should be a road map, providing direction to the company. Without it, the organization can wander from initiative to initiative, losing its ability to navigate what is working and what isn't. The task of developing strategic alignment can be daunting. The reasons for this vary, but the most common are the following:

Poorly defined strategy: Some organizations have very broad and ill-defined strategic directions. I am reminded of a situation in which an organization wanted to "create sustainability over the next ten years." This very broad statement was difficult to measure and define. When pushed, the leadership team had very different perspectives of what the statement meant. When organizations use such broad and open-ended statements, it is difficult to pin down the key actions and behaviors that will be required to deliver results.

Marginal goals: Some organizations define their strategy solely based on financial goals, such as gross margin improvement of X%, increase wallet share by X%, and increase revenue by X %. These types of goal statements offer no clear direction to the workforce relative to specific actions to take and they leave open the question of which behaviors are acceptable and required to achieve success.

Lofty mission statements: Strategy is sometimes stated in terms of a mission or vision statement. Lofty vision statements that use broad words can be interpreted to mean a variety of things to different constituents. It is difficult to create concrete workforce alignment without further analysis. Examples might be, "We are the customer's first choice for X," "We are the employer of choice in our field," or "We are the global provider of X services." These are great statements, but they're unclear.

What do employees need to do every day to deliver on these statements? One organization I worked with took the time to define "global" from a customer-, process-, and leadership-behavior perspective. This helped define the mission statement greatly.

Forgotten values: Values are stated somewhere, but they are often not included in the talent system or not defined in behavioral terms. Other competencies are used for assessing talent and people are not evaluated for acting in concert with the company's stated values.

Do any of these common issues sound familiar? If they do, you are not alone. Many organizations have ill-defined strategies. Sometimes they exist solely in the leader's head or are understood by the leadership team, but not written down in a coherent fashion. This is not because these organizations are bad or ineffective. It is often because their leaders are moving so fast that they fail to get the basic underpinnings spelled out clearly and simply for everyone to understand. This can be a real opportunity for talent and other human resources people if you have a receptive leadership team that believes talent is a key competitive advantage. In *Optimizing Talent* (Sharkey and Eccher, 2010), we included an initial discussion of what leaders do that supports talent efforts. The previous chapter also outlines the behaviors required. Taking our Optimizing Talent Survey will help you gauge your leaders' willingness to step into strategic alignment work. The link to the survey is in Chapter One, and it is a very good place to start your diagnosis.

Key Steps to Making Strategy Actionable in Talent Terms

The great news is that all of these common issues can be resolved if you have the leadership engagement to do so. However, there can be significant challenges if your leadership team is strictly focused on the financial goals. Don't despair. It can be done! You can use the same approaches offered here, though it just may be a bit more difficult to execute them with a leader or leadership team that is solely focused on numbers. The first thing to do is to decide your point of entry and follow the steps outlined below.

Step 1: Conduct an Analysis of the Organization's Key Messages

Look for the clues the organization gives you relative to what is expected from leaders and employees from a behavioral standpoint.

List these items: values, mission statement, numbers, strategic imperatives, goals, strategy documents, etc.

Exercise 4.1: Analysis of Key Messages

1. *Which of these documents or concepts is most important to the leaders? Specifically, where do leaders spend most of their energy in communications: presentations, board reports, or investor communications? Examples of particular focus in these areas include such concepts as quality products and services, customer care, teamwork, efficiency, etc.*

   _____

   _____

   _____

2. *Underscore the words that leaders use the most to describe the business needs and direction.*

_____

_____

_____

3. *Select three or no more than four concepts that are important. If you are using the values statement again, narrow it down to the values that are the most non-negotiable in the company.*

_____

_____

_____

4. *If you have done the culture analysis discussed in the previous chapter, refer to the ideal and select the behaviors that either need to change or align with the ones you underscored above.*

_____

_____

_____

With this analysis done you are ready to move to the next step.

Step 2: *Define the Key Behaviors*

There are several approaches to Step 2. I usually advocate for one of two approaches:

Approach A

For the items you have underscored as most important to your leaders, craft a series of interview questions to engage them in defining 1) what these items look like from a behavioral point of view, or 2) what the concepts look like when they are being performed optimally. Ask the leaders to give you examples of peak performance around the concepts. Example: When we are really customer-focused, our employees are doing X. Be sure your questions are focused and asked in business terms and "HR speak." Engage enough leaders in this process to get a clear picture of what resonates with them. Approach A is the preferred approach. However, if you cannot use Approach A, go to Approach B.

Approach B

Create a "straw dog" from the various reviews you have done in Steps 1 and 2. The straw dog would include the most important behaviors for business success and an articulation of how to recognize those behaviors in action. Particularly important is what the behaviors look like at peak performance. Share the draft document with key leaders following a similar process. This is often a quicker method, but be careful. It can release leaders and stakeholders from making critical decisions about expected behaviors for business success, but you also run the risk of leaders not taking personal accountability for behavior change. However, we have seen this approach work well depending on the environment and on how much dialogue the stakeholders have relative to the topic. If you use Approach B, you will need to adjust the steps below accordingly. For example, you still want to engage your business leader and share the document you created with the key stakeholders. Decide on the best way to do that and then capture their feedback on what you have prepared,

Exercise 4.2: Key Behaviors

1. *List the questions you will ask your leaders to help define these concepts in behavioral terms.*

_____

_____

_____

2. *Draft your "straw dog" by listing the four or five interview questions you will ask your leaders. This will help you to gain clarity around the behaviors that they think are important.*

_____

_____

_____

*Note: If you ask too many questions, you will lose the attention of busy executives. Narrow your questions to the critical few.

Step 3: *Enroll your primary business leader*

Meet with your leader, whether it is the CEO or a business partner, to review your analysis. Validate the most important questions and check if any others should be included. Ask the leader the questions you have listed; then interview the key stakeholders. Check with your business partner as to which key stakeholders should be included in the interviews or have input into the draft document. If you have done a good analysis and you have data for the ideal culture, you should be able to have some compelling and educational discussions with the leadership team. Here are the actions for Step 3 in a nutshell.

1. *Agree on a data collection method.*

2. *Agree on how the initiative will be introduced to the rest of the leaders.*

3. *Decide key stakeholders*

Step 4: *Launch the data collection/validation process*

Communicate with your stakeholders so that they know what you are doing and what will be expected of them. Be sure that this is a joint communication from you and your primary business leader or partner. Communication can take place in a number of ways. Below is a list of how you might communicate the effort:

1. *Have a staff meeting with the business leader.*

2. Send a written email outlining objective.

3. Do both of the above.

Be sure to include the expectations of the interviewees, how much time is involved, and so on.

Exercise 4.3: Approach and Key Messages

Write your approach and key messages below.

_____

_____

_____

_____

_____

_____

_____

Step 5: *Collect the data*

Lay out your data collection plan. Four methods are suggested. The degree of openness and candor of those you interview will determine your data collection method. Pick the method that best suits your organization culture or dynamics:

1. *Method 1 – Facilitate a meeting with the entire team. An exercise is offered in* Optimizing Talent *that you can modify. List the questions; have the leaders use brainstorming techniques to answer the questions. This is the optimal method when there is a high degree of candor.*

2. *Method 2 – Conduct interviews of each person. Ensure that people know the interview answers are anonymous, but not confidential. This method is optimal when there may be trust issues among the stakeholders.*

3. *Method 3 – Create a survey. Have each leader fill it out and return it to you. This approach is optimal when trust issues might exist or when there are time constraints. Obviously, surveys take more time. The data obtained with this method are sometimes not as rich and this builds less engagement, but it may be the approach that best suits your organization.*

4. *Method 4 – Follow up a survey with targeted interviews or a meeting to clarify the survey results. In time-constrained organizations, this can be difficult to organize. You can send the survey results out to the respondents and ask for validation or clarification.*

**Step 6**: Conduct your analysis

Analyze the data and develop a clear template of the three to five behaviors that are essential for business success. Use the template to create the draft document of your analysis. Share it with those whom you interviewed or surveyed and get their final sign off.

**Step 7**: Create your talent assessment document and approach

Now you are ready to create a survey and interview protocol with which to assess your talent against the behaviors that are most important for business success. Directions for using this assessment document are provided in Chapter Five.

There are resources available to you that will help you to create solid, identifiable traits for each behavior that is important for success. I recommend _FYI: For Your Improvement_ by Michael Lombardo and Robert Eichinger.

**Step 8**: Ensure talent brand alignment

The final step in ensuring strategic alignment is to review your talent brand proposition as discussed in Chapter Two. Make sure that there is consistency between what you are saying relative to the expected behavior and culture of the organization internally and that your external documents and approaches to attracting talent mirror your internal message.

Chapter Four Checklist

Before you move to the next section of this workbook, go through the checklist below to ensure that you have the necessary information and data to be successful in assessing talent. If you answer "yes" to most of the questions, move forward. If you can only answer "yes" to 50% of the questions, we suggest you go back and try to increase your effectiveness using the guidelines outlined in this chapter. Strategic alignment is, after all, the bedrock for all talent initiatives going forward. Remember though, that making sure you have great talent is a journey that will take you several years to perfect. Also, you will need to continually review your plans and adjust them to reflect ever-changing business dynamics as well as creating an influx of increasing globalization.

- ☐ Are you clear on the most critical behaviors necessary to drive business outcomes?
- ☐ Are these behaviors derived from key business imperatives (goals, strategy, vision, mission, values, etc.)?
- ☐ Have you defined these behaviors in simple terms that everyone can understand and with which everyone can identify?
- ☐ Do you have key stakeholder buy-in and sign-off?
- ☐ Do you have a document that is available to use to assess and develop talent in the rest of the Talent Optimization Framework™?
- ☐ Do you have a communication plan for engaging the rest of the workforce?

Summary

If you have worked through this section and answered the questions in the checklist to a 75% level of confidence, proceed to the next chapter. Remember that communication to the rest of the workforce will be very important. Or, if you were lucky enough to secure culture and leadership alignment as outlined in Chapter Three, then you are ready to move to the next section of this workbook. Remember, you may have to take elements from both Chapter Three and this chapter to move forward.

As a parting thought, these steps should be a part of all business leaders' conversations and discussions of expectations with the employees they lead. If you follow the above recipe, this will become a natural act for the business leaders you engaged in this important work. Helping them become expert communicators around key behaviors can be a great coaching role for you as a talent professional. We recommend you read *Communicating for Change* by Roger D'Aprix (1996), a classic book that remains relevant because it speaks to what employees anywhere in the world need to hear from their leaders.

CHAPTER FIVE

TALENT ASSESSMENT

by Dan Martin

There are many ways to assess talent at the organizational, individual, and team levels. However, GE has long been the benchmark that other organizations use. Many organizations have adapted the tools and techniques of GE to their own culture and context. This chapter gives you a deeper insight into GE's Talent Assessment process. We deliberately decided to focus this chapters as a "case study" of the GE process because of the expertise that authors have with it. When exploring this process, it's important to remember that not one size fits all. For example, HP used a 4 Box rather than a 9 Box to assess talent; others use top, middle, and bottom for assessments. As you read this chapter, take this information and incorporate it into your own company's strategy and use your own company language to create your assessment process.

Exercise 5.1: Getting Started

1. *How do you identify top talent today? What is your current method for understanding the vitality of the workforce and differentiating talent? How do you assess potential?*

_____

_____

_____

_____

_____

2. Do you have succession plans for key roles? How do you currently assess individuals identified as top talent/backup candidates for key roles?

_____

_____

_____

_____

_____

_____

3. Do you have a process for interviewing top talent and providing them with feedback on their developmental needs that includes development action planning? How do you track their progress?

_____

_____

_____

_____

_____

_____

GE's Session C Process of Talent Assessment

GE's Session C Process is a formal multilevel review of organizational performance, talent assessment, and succession planning that ensures optimal organizational alignment. It is an intimate and systemic process that is conducted annually. A variety of tools is used to this end, such as the formal Session C meeting during which there is an active dialogue regarding the performance and promotability of every employee. The Session C process is used to assess and identify top talent for talent assessment interviews.

Talent assessment interviews are part of GE's overall talent assessment review process and they are completed for a select group of talented individuals who deserve special attention. These interviews provide in-depth knowledge of the talent pool and a systemic rhythm of assessment reviews, which is the foundation for creating a steady, self-renewing stream of talented leaders for all levels of the organization.

In addition, employees are rated and ranked on a nine vitality matrix called the Nine Block. The desired outcome of the Nine Block is to improve the overall talent pool of the organization and to continue to identify future leaders. In his book, GE's former senior vice president for human resources, Bill Conaty, lists talent assessment as one of the seven key principles of being a "Talent Master." (Conaty & Charan, 2010)

Principles of the Talent Masters

Rigorous talent assessments are one of the crucial elements of a world-class talent system. Talent masters have the same goal and results orientation in their people processes as they do in their financial systems. They set explicit time-based people development goals and discuss the why and how of these goals. They review people as thoroughly and regularly as they review operations, business performance, strategy, and budgets. Crucially, they integrate the people reviews with each of the others, gathering and updating the information as the person progresses. Like the financial systems, the people systems have rhythm and rigor, and evolve over time as new needs arise. (Conaty & Charan, 2010)

As the talent pool of employees and leaders continues to grow and develop, their value to the organization also grows exponentially as they take on larger and more impactful roles. The process requires a systematic approach to providing employee feedback and development action planning. The feedback is a year-long collaborative process between an employee and manager that links observable results and behaviors to the goals of the work unit and the strategic and operational processes of the business. The top talents are scheduled for a talent assessment interview as part of their development action plan using behavioral interview techniques like the ones described in the books *The Evaluation Interview: How to Probe Deeply, Get Candid Answers*, and *Predict the Performance of Job Candidates* (Fear and Chiron, 2002) and T*opgrading: The Proven Hiring and Promoting Method that Turbocharges Company Performance* (3rd ed., Smart, 2012).

Steps of the Talent Assessment Process

The talent assessment process is made up of the following steps. Use your own list of behaviors derived in Chapter Four in the process outlined below.

1. *Business leader and human resources manager (HRM) recommend candidates through the overall talent assessment review process similar to GE's Session C process. The top talent in the organization is identified using the Nine-Block rating and ranking matrix.*

2. *Trained assessors are assigned in pairs with one assigned as the lead coach to conduct the assessment interview and prepare a formal report on each top talent individual identified.*

3. *The HRM notifies the selected assessee's manager and business or functional leader.*

4. *The HRM emails a congratulatory letter to the assessee.*

5. *Upon confirmed participation, the assessee provides a list of five to six potential internal reference checks and a copy of his or her resume and latest performance review.*

6. *HRM schedules reference checks and interviews using paired trained assessors and feedback session assessee and assessors.*

7. *Assessors prepare for the assessment interview by reviewing the resume and latest performance review and finalizing questions. The assessee is called to explain the process and answer questions.*

8. *Assessors conduct the interview (approximately two hours), then summarize interview notes and identify areas for further probing with reference checks.*

9. *Assessors collaborate and prepare draft of the Leadership Assessment Report.*

10. *One of the assessors is assigned as the coach. This assessor conducts a feedback session and revises the Leadership Assessment Report to incorporate any changes or modifications.*

11. *The assessor sends the final Leadership Assessment Report to a limited distribution (assessee, assessee's HRM, direct manager, business or functional leader, global HR leader, and any other appropriate HR leaders).*

12. *Development Action Plans are monitored through the overall talent assessment review process.*

FIG 5.1: EMPLOYEE DIFFERENTIATION PROCESS

EMPLOYEE RATING NINE BLOCK

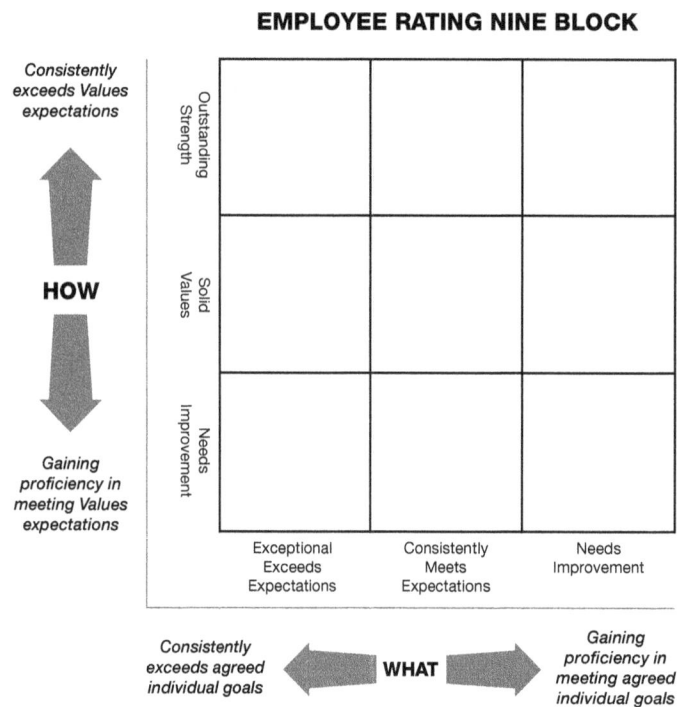

The operational definition of the overall rating of the employee is based on the following criteria. See Figure 5.1.

1. *The overall assessment of the employee's contribution to the organization*

2. *The objective view of past performance, demonstrated values, and unique skills*

3. *The guidelines available to ensure appropriate differentiation across the business*

FIG 5.2: EMPLOYEE DIFFERENTIATION PROCESS
OVERALL RATING

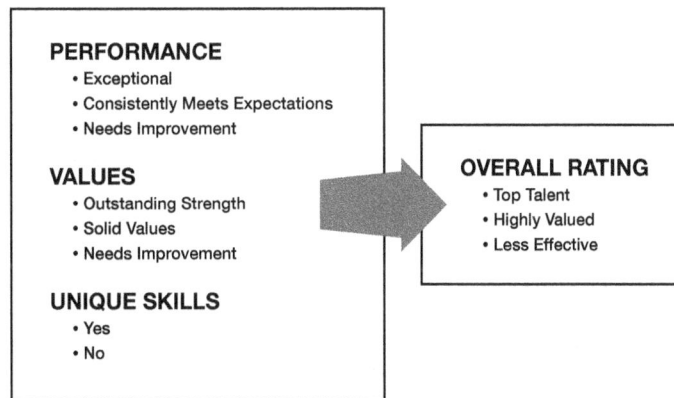

PERFORMANCE
- Exceptional
- Consistently Meets Expectations
- Needs Improvement

VALUES
- Outstanding Strength
- Solid Values
- Needs Improvement

UNIQUE SKILLS
- Yes
- No

OVERALL RATING
- Top Talent
- Highly Valued
- Less Effective

Top Talent: Represents the very best contributors within the organization. These individuals consistently perform and demonstrate values at a level that strongly differentiates their contributions. These individuals are recognized to be at an additional level of capability and performance.

Highly Valued: Represents the strength of the organization. These individuals consistently perform at a level that strongly supports business performance and values. They are highly capable and high-achieving performers who are recognized for their contributions within the organization.

Less Effective: Represents the least effective contributors within the organization. These individuals are not always able to contribute at a desire level. There is a need for change, and generally those in this category need to improve performance and/or values with an action plan.

The operational definition of the promotability of the employee is based on the following criteria.

1. *Demonstrates capacity based on performance, aptitude, ability, and an interest in taking on broader responsibilities*

2. *Demonstrates attributes that could be applied to bigger roles*

3. *Demonstrates leadership capabilities*

4. *Demonstrates communication and influence skills*

High Potential: These individuals continually expand their personal capabilities and independently take on greater responsibility. There is a high probability of competing successfully for higher-banded positions. These individuals demonstrate the capability to move up at least one salary band (or to a position with significantly greater breadth and impact) and to attain significant additional progression thereafter.

Moderate Potential: These individuals continually expand personal capabilities and demonstrate willingness to take on greater responsibility. These individuals will likely compete successfully for a higher-banded position or take a job at the same band with broader responsibilities.

Limited-Topped Out: These individuals are performing professionals/experts, and are likely to remain in their position or move laterally within the same band with similar responsibilities/depth. These individuals are positioned at the appropriate level to maximize their effectiveness. Please remember that this is a feedback and development process, not a "rank-and-yank" process that we have seen companies use.

FIG. 5.3: EMPLOYEE RANKING NINE BLOCK

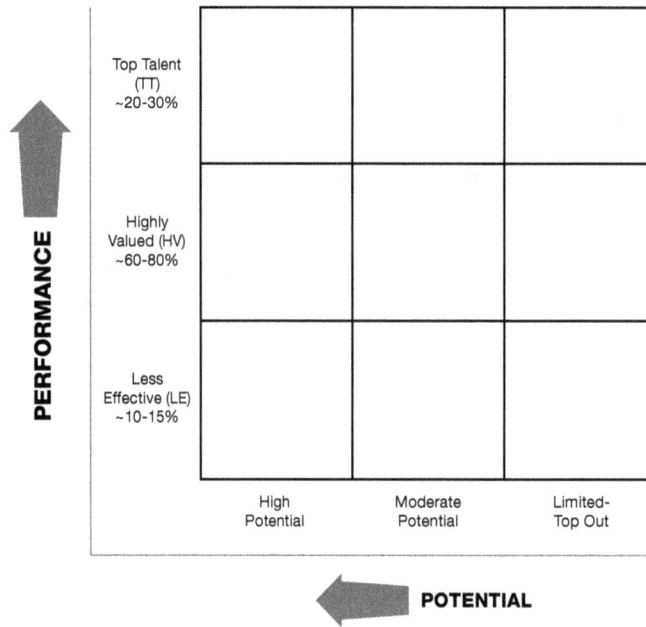

FIG 5.4: TALENT POOL

FOUNDATION ✚ GROWTH

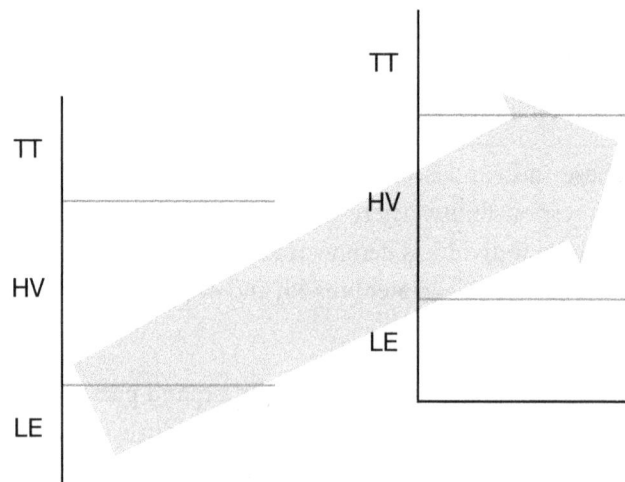

Assessment Interview Guide

The assessment interview should take approximately two hours. Make clear this is not a job interview, but a career aid. If necessary, return to topics that need to be explored further. The sentences below are a guide, not a script. Look for patterns of behavior and leadership traits that are important to the organization. Feel free to add additional questions if needed. Listen and let the candidate talk, downplay any negative information, and be supportive and friendly.

We cannot stress enough the importance of having a thorough assessment of talent. Without it, you have no way of assuring that you have a consistent method and approach for determining the talent in your organization. A consistent assessment process aligned with the business strategy and key behaviors creates a common understanding and framework ensuring that everyone will assess their talent in the same way. This way you can be sure that top talent in one business unit is similar to or of the same quality as top talent in another business unit. A crisp and consistent assessment is the launch pad of the rest of your talent system. It provides the rationale for the top talent, while also helping define your succession, recruitment, and development strategies. Equally important, it becomes the baseline for a systematic measurement of improvements needed to do the data analytics discussed in Chapter Ten.

See the Appendix for the Sample Assessment Interview. Remember use these steps, but build your own guide based on the key behaviors determined for your organization. A sample assessment interview consists of the following components:

- Look for evidence of the expected leadership behaviors and values

- A thorough understanding of the person, i.e., family background, role models, etc.

- Education and training

- Work history and experience

- Self-assessment of strengths and development areas

- Plans and goals for the future

- Reference checking model and questions

Chapter Five Checklist

Before moving onto Chapter Six, review the following chapter to ensure that you have a good talent assessment plan in place.

☐ Do you have a clear plan for assessing your talent?

☐ Are you clear on the specific areas—skills and behaviors—against which you need to assess talent?

☐ Do you have a systematic process and tools in place for consistent assessment?

☐ Have you articulated what "best" looks like for the organization as well as "good" and "poor," and have you spelled this out in clear and observable terms?

☐ Do you have trained internal human resources talent to conduct an unbiased assessment?

☐ Can you aggregate the assessment data to provide a compelling and actionable picture for the organization to use as the basis for improvement plans?

Summary

The talent assessment process is a continuous improvement process. Its purpose is to identify and develop top leadership talent and it includes a talent assessment interview as a developmental tool in which the organization's top talent receives special insight and coaching to help them improve. As a result of this process, the organization continues to grow its pool of top talent and to improve its succession-planning process. This process will provide you with a solid understanding of the skills and behavioral depth of your talent succession pools. It also helps you to quickly focus on the developmental areas needed to get the talent pool ready for the next assignment. Done well, assessment provides laser focus on developmental gaps and also provides the baseline from which to measure talent pool readiness and improvement, which we will discuss more in Chapters Nine and Ten.

Using this process sets you up for the rest of the implementation of the Talent Optimization Framework™. In particular, it provides a thorough overview of the organization's development gaps. Having moved through the process this far means that you can now aggregate the assessment data at the organization level. You have a clear picture of the strengths you can leverage and the skills and behavioral gaps that need to be filled through the variety of interventions discussed in the next chapters. Note that you will be able to create an overall development roadmap for your organization to include coaching, learning experiences, programs, and developmental assignments. You are now able to see gaps in particular departments and can do the same developmental roadmaps for subsets of the organization and respective teams. You also have individual development plans for your top talent. We might add that this step gives you the opportunity to have development plans for all your talent, not just your top talent. Finally, the linkage to performance management is a key step to help others understand their strengths and areas for improvement to increase their overall effectiveness.

CHAPTER SIX

PERFORMANCE MANAGEMENT

by Phil Dixon

The Fallacy (and Conundrums) of the Current Systems:
How Do You Know If You Have It Right?

The most likely answer is that you probably don't! Years ago, W. Edwards Deming (1982) advocated the removal of barriers that rob hourly workers of their pride of workmanship. Among other things, "This implies the abolition of the annual merit rating system (performance appraisals) and of management by objectives. Again, the responsibility of managers, supervisors, and foremen must be changed from sheer numbers to quality." When asked what should replace performance appraisals in the workplace, Deming said simply "Try leadership."

Nothing has improved since Deming wrote these words. Indeed, if anything, matters may have become worse. During the past two decades, performance management systems have become ubiquitous in most large companies. Although recent trends indicate that a few more far-sighted companies are abolishing the process (Bersin, 2013), various researchers estimate that 90%-95% of companies of any significant size have a performance management system.

Performance management systems, as they are currently constructed and implemented, do not work. Period. Why organizations spend time and money on such demoralizing systems is unfathomable to us. Just ask any manager or employee how he or she feels when he or she hears the words "annual review" or "focal review time," and you will get a sense of the amount of loathing there is for the process at all levels of the organization.

Let's focus for a moment on the underlying research. Bracken et al (2001), in reviewing the vast amount of literature on this subject, state that the opinion that one arrives at concerning the use of performance appraisal systems is a little like "the blind men groping an elephant, each arriving at a different conclusion depending on their angle."

Kluger and Denisi (1996, 2000) are more direct. The results of their meta-analysis indicate that not only are performance appraisals not effective, in 38% of the studies reviewed, they actually made the performance of the individual worse. In big round numbers, 30% of the time performance appraisals were effective in improving performance, 30% of the time they had no impact, and 40% of the time they made performance worse.

Our experience and research indicate that people don't need much feedback for what they need to improve upon. Indeed, approximately 80% of the time, people know what they need to work on, but for whatever reason, they just have not done so. They would be better served if managers focused on helping them with what they already know they need to work on. This is called coaching.

Coens and Jenkins (2002) are also very direct. They state something that is intuitively obvious to most of us: coaching and development conversations are much more powerful than criticism as they motivate and encourage people based on what they are doing right.

In general, performance management systems as they are currently implemented do not create meaningful dialogue and focus. Wouldn't it be better for managers and leaders to simply be clear about what is expected, and then engage in effective, regular, evaluative conversation rather than fall back on an annual form and technology-based process? (See Exhibit 6.1 for a detailed list of performance review components and Exhibit 6.2 for a sample development discussion form.)

Exhibit 6.1: Performance Review Components

Please allow us to begin with a few words of caution or explanation:

- Not all of the components we describe below are applicable in all situations. While we are describing some of the best practices that we know about, not all best practices are applicable in all cases. Our purpose here is to assist you in becoming a more reflective practitioner.

- Not all of the components are of equal weight in all organizations. The weightings will change.

- The list is deliberately a mix of statements and questions.

- We use the word manager as synonymous with the person who is determining and delivering the performance review, and the word subordinate for the recipient of the review. We know that this wording is not used 100% of the time, but it appears to be understood in the majority of instances.

A. *The organizational context*

1. The organization must, in general, be a high-trust, low-political environment.

2. The company culture needs to be supportive of growth and candid feedback.

3. The leaders of the organization must, themselves, be role models; they need to be reviewed and be seen to change as a result of that review.

B. *The performance review system*

1. The performance review system needs to be separate from the compensation, remuneration, or bonus systems. In addition, there needs to be honest clarity of purpose – i.e., is the system really developmental or is it simply a means of determining compensation or positioning for other purposes?

2. Whatever the system, it has to be seen to be executed in an effective manner.

3. The system itself must not be time-consuming – for manager or employee; the conversation resulting from the system should take as much time as is required.

4. Annual review systems tend to be focused on the more recent activities of the individual – in today's fast-moving and complex environment, who can remember what we were doing one year ago? If an annual system is to be at all effective, it must have a mechanism for collecting past data.

5. Is the system just being used as a mask for poor management/leadership and/or poor management/leadership training?

C. *The performance review environment*

1. Is the current organizational context relatively stable? If there have been significant changes, are they seen as positive? If there have been recent layoffs, or some other significant event, don't hold the performance reviews.

2. What has the recent performance of the company been?

3. What about re-organizations, restructuring? What about a new boss, promotions, team reassignments, etc.?

4. Is there a defined, effective, and trained coaching model within the organization that aligns with and supports the performance review process?

5. Do the other HR and company systems align with the performance review process?

6. Are the keepers and monitors of the process (typically HR) trusted?

D. *The manager*

1. Has the manager been trained in the need to have regular, ongoing performance conversations?

2. Have these been occurring?

3. Are these regular conversations part of the manager's performance review and bonus?

4. Has the manager been trained in how to have performance improvement conversations?

5. Is there a trusted and credible relationship between the manager and the subordinate?

6. Is the manager seen as biased?

7. Is the manager seen as informed?

8. Has the manager sought out others' opinions about the subordinate?

9. Does the manager have the courage to state his or her own opinions rather than hide behind those of others?

10. Has the manager prepared for the conversation?

11. Does the manager understand the aspirations, goals, and makeup of the recipient?

12. Has the manager been trained in how people change (or not) after feedback?

13. Has the manager been trained on how to coach?

14. Has the manager been trained in how to have career conversations? Does he or she hold them?

15. Has the manager been trained in how to recognize and/or ask about what else is going on in the subordinate's life and alter the timing of the review if necessary?

16. Do managers always take enough preparation time for the performance review process for each of their subordinates?

E. *The performance review form*

1. The form should be completed by the subordinate before the manager.

2. The form needs to be brief – we recommend one page at the maximum.

3. The form needs to be easy to use and understand; no complex language, explanations, or competency lists.

4. The form needs to reflect a developmental focus.

5. The form should include an area for a career goal discussion for the subordinate together with an area for ONE short-term focus or step towards that goal.

6. The form should have room to identify between 3 and 5 strengths exhibited by the subordinate.

7. The form should request ONE developmental area.

8. There should be a discussion area to link the subordinate's strengths to his or her development area.

9. There should be a discussion area to link the subordinate's developmental area to his or her short-term career goal step.

F. *The performance review event*

1. The subordinate needs to be involved in setting the time and place of the performance review discussion.

2. The discussion should take place in private and on "neutral" ground – not the manager's office.

3. The performance review discussion always takes place in two parts. The first is delivery and discussion of the data; then there is the discussion about what the subordinate plans to do as a result of the discussion. There is time in between these two portions for the subordinate to reflect on what he or she wishes to do.

G. The subordinate

    1. Has the subordinate been trained or given coaching on how to receive feedback?

    2. Has the subordinate been trained or given coaching on how to change as a result of feedback?

    3. What else is going on in the work and home/social life of the participant ?

    4. Does the subordinate tend to have a positivity bias or a negativity bias?

    5. Does the subordinate tend to have a fixed ("I know") or growth ("I can learn") mindset?

    6. Has the subordinate been able to demonstrate learning and change in the past?

H. The feedback content

    1. Are narrative comments clear, focused, and actionable?

    2. Are narrative comments limited in number?

    3. The content needs to be structured in a way that encourages discussion, conversation, and enquiry rather than simply ratings, numbers, or grades.

    4. The discussion needs to focus on a single goal.

    5. Feedback needs to address the "self" conundrums outlined above – i.e., if there are "self" or behavioral issues, then the manager needs to be doubly clear on the best manner to get those across.

    6. If the feedback is about "self," is that ability or behavior related to a task or goal that is important to the subordinate?

    7. The content needs to address the performance of the subordinate against a pre-determined profile or set of goals. It is tough to "measure up" if the goal posts are not clear.

    8. The feedback content needs to align with the recipient's sense of self or desired future.

I. Follow-up

    1. Whatever the agreement about goals and progress during a performance review session, there needs to be regular follow-up. Some research suggests that 70% of managers never follow-up when an employee has been given feedback.

    2. Managers are able to get third-party assistance (e.g., internal, peer, or external coaching, training programs, etc.) if required for the subordinate to achieve the goal that has been set.

J. Brain-friendly process

This component is written slightly differently in two ways.

    1. There are no specific questions or checks that follow.

2. It reflects across all of the other components.

Check all aspects of the performance review system based upon the commentary in Section A.

Exhibit 6.2: Sample Development Discussion Form

Employee _____

Manager _____

Date _____

Period Covered _____

Review of this last period

Please summarize what you set out to do this period:

_____
_____
_____

Please summarize what you achieved:

_____
_____
_____

Please summarize the extra work that came your way:

_____
_____
_____

Please list three or four strengths that you exercised this period:

_____
_____
_____

Please list additional strengths that you have that were not used during this period:

_____
_____
_____

Some Conundrums

Given that there is a significant chance that the feedback given within a performance review system will have no effect or might do damage, it would be good to know what will cause the feedback to be part of the 30% that has a positive impact. There are, however, a number of conundrums.

The first is that there are so many variables to take into account; whether performance appraisal systems are effective or ineffective, the reasons behind the result are elusive (Bracken, et al 2001).

The next conundrum has two parts. Kluger and DeNisi (2000) start the investigation of what works and what doesn't work when giving feedback by offering us a taxonomy of feedback. They suggest that there are three layers of feedback: 1) feedback about self, 2) feedback about task, and 3) feedback about task detail. Their hypothesis is that feedback about task is most likely to work, whereas feedback about self and task detail will not.

Hogan and Hogan (2010) state that 75% of the employees in corporate America report that the biggest stressor in their work lives is their boss. In addition, they report various estimates that between 35% and 60% of managers will fail or become derailed within the next five years. In both instances, the reason for this is "over-riding personality defects" – just the area where one would assume that feedback would be useful. But Kluger and DeNisi caution that feedback about self doesn't work. Conundrum!

The third conundrum again has two parts. The feedback within a performance review tends to have two components: the rating, or quantitative component, and the narrative or qualitative component. Smither & Walker (2004), reporting on work by Ferstl and Bruskiewicz, (2000), suggest that recipients tend to pay more attention to the qualitative component than to the quantitative. We did an analysis of over 1000 units of qualitative feedback between managers in a high-tech company in Silicon Valley and found that a full two-thirds of the qualitative feedback was about 'the self' – exactly the domain that Kluger and DeNisi suggest doesn't work. Conundrum!

The final conundrum involves the very essence of annual (or periodic) systems. A significant body of research shows that for feedback to be effective, it has to be delivered in a timely manner with respect to the action that caused the feedback to arise. If the feedback is not timely, then give up hope for much performance improvement. Conundrum!

So Let's Stop Doing Performance Appraisals!

When we have spoken to HR professionals in connection with the discontinuation of their performance appraisal systems, they typically respond with a statement about the requirement to continuously document performance in case there is a need for their company to defend itself against litigious employees and managers who have acted inappropriately. Yet, if we then ask the corporate lawyers how effective the system was in helping the defense against litigation, the majority of them say that the information contained in the performance appraisal reports was more damaging to their case than helpful.

Litigious employees are an extreme minority. Should we continue systems that are expensive in terms of money, time, effort, and psychological stress just to deal with that minority rather than put in place systems that would energize and motivate the majority? Many of the systems are in place simply to ensure that managers have at least one performance-related conversation with their employees per year. This seems to us to be a management or management training issue rather than a desired outcome of a performance management system. Managers and employees both fail to see the day-to-day value of these exercises.

A Brain-friendly Approach (Dixon et al, 2010; Gordon 2012)

There are five important principles that drive how the brain works which will help explain why people are often averse to feedback:

1) As human beings, we drive towards safety and reward (real and perceived) and away from threat and danger (real or perceived). When our brain is in a threatened state, our ability to listen, learn, and change is severely limited.

2) The brain has two modes of processing, conscious and non-conscious, and the ratio between the two (although not accurately measured) is approximately 1:1,000,000 in how we handle cues and signals, i.e., the non-conscious has a much greater sway in our reactions.

3) Human beings don't necessarily react rationally.

4) There are many cues and signals that can put us into a threat state or a reward state There are some general threats (outlined below), as well as those which are specific to each individual, such as biases, triggers, and patterns. There are, however, too many of these to cover in this chapter. Managers who get to know their subordinates are likely to understand some of these. Managers who don't will run into them with unpredictable results.

5) Stress has more of an impact than we ever thought. It causes us to lose sleep and lowers our positivity and resilience. It weakens our immune system and it can cause us to focus on the negative and lose sight of the big picture.

Research shows that it is the very act of feedback rather than whether it is positive or negative that causes the brain to react in fear. This is because the concept and act of feedback are threatening. For example, simply saying to someone, "Let me give you some feedback," can put their brain into a threat state. Simply the knowledge that a person might have to have a meeting with a manager can be threatening. Knowing that I have to meet with someone for my performance review will probably give me "anticipatory stress."

Some of the Ways that Our Brains Feel Threatened

1) The brain likes security: it perceives all change as a threat and craves certainty and consistency. If any of these are challenged, then the act that causes that challenge will be seen as a threat. For example, the very fact that a subordinate does not know what is going to be in his/her review will put his/her brain into a threat state.

2) None of us likes to be told what to do, and all of us like to have some control over our own lives and destiny. In other words, we like our autonomy. If the feedback process, event, content, or conversation comes across as "you should," then often we will nod politely, but non-consciously reject the feedback. For many people, if the feedback indicates, "You should do this,"

then that will be perceived as a threat. If we select a change for ourselves, then we feel differently about it.

3) We all want fairness in the way we are treated. The brain is exquisite at identifying fair and unfair treatment. If we do not see feedback as fair, then we will reject it, again probably non-consciously. For example, if someone is given feedback about a certain behavior, but she sees other people behaving the same way, this will be seen as unfair. This will be even more egregious if the manager is the person who is seen doing that behavior.

4) All of us want to keep our esteem intact. If a person hears that he has failed to achieve a goal, or told that he is wrong, he is likely to (at the very least non-consciously) interpret this as a threat to his esteem. We constantly judge ourselves against others, and if someone tells us that we are other than perfect, even though at some level we sense that it might be true, we feel threatened.

5) If the feedback impacts the trust between us and another person, then we feel threatened. If it threatens our trust in the environment around us or our self-trust, again, we feel threatened.

These are some general areas that seem to apply to most people. The weighting and relevance of all of these is highly personal; however, all of these will obstruct performance feedback from being received in such a manner that it can be acted upon.

There are other factors, such as individual biases, triggers, and patterns, that cause feedback to be accepted or rejected. Furthermore, just the use of some words can be threatening, even thought there was no intent to threaten. For example, "Don't be worried," is likely to be interpreted as a threat. Indeed, the phrase "performance review" triggers a threat state for many people!

Further Analysis

There are many reasons why performance management systems are seen to be ineffective. We have identified over 50 separate factors that have to be aligned in order for the appraisal and feedback process to be truly effective. They relate to the following ten major aspects:

1. *The organizational context*

2. *The performance review system itself*

3. *The performance review environment*

4. *The manager*

5. *The performance review form*

6. *The performance review event*

7. *The subordinate*

8. *The feedback content*

9. *Follow-up*

10. *Brain-friendly process*

We will look at these areas more closely, but first let's step back and reconsider the purpose of performance appraisal systems, in general, and feedback, in particular. To begin, we think it is reasonable to assume that the overall intent of performance appraisal is: …to create sustainable skill development, task focus, or behavior change at either an organizational, team, or individual level. How are you defining the purpose of your performance review process? Write your current definition. How does it differ from the above definition?

_____

_____

We encourage you to use this as a working definition of a successful performance appraisal system. You can then judge each of the various elements that we expand upon below as to whether they move you toward your success objective or not.

In all of our research, one thing stands out: There needs to be a trusted and credible relationship between the manager and the subordinate for any performance review process to be effective. If this relationship is not present, then the rest of the system becomes almost irrelevant. For further analysis of your current performance management system, we encourage you to look at Exercises 6.1 and 6.2. Because these are lengthy exercises, we have put them in the Appendix. Please do them before moving on to Exercise 6.3.

Exercise 6.3: Looking to the Future

1. Please briefly describe your career goals for the next three to five years.

_____

_____

2. Please identify ONE step that you would like take over the next period to move towards those career goals.

_____

_____

3. Please identify ONE development area that you believe you should work on this year.

_____

_____

4. Please briefly explain how you could use your strengths to assist in learning this new area.

_____

_____

5. Please briefly explain how the addition of this development area will assist you in achieving your career step for this period.

_____

_____

6) Add any other comments that you wish to make about your work at this company.

_____

_____

Do the test again. Wait for a few months after a new process has been introduced and repeat the test that we referred to above. Ask managers and employees what they think of the coaching and performance process. We think you will be astonished at the results. You will see that a coaching approach will reverberate in the market and people will be knocking on your door to join your organization because you are reinforcing your brand as a great place to build talent!

Chapter Six Checklist

- ☐ Are you clear on the goals for your current performance management system?
- ☐ Have you developed specific goals for your new performance management system?
- ☐ Have you reviewed your current system for brain-friendly approaches?
- ☐ Are the behaviors that are expected in your organization spelled out clearly and are they included in your feedback and review process?
- ☐ Are your leaders in support of the process, and do they understand their role in ensuring it is effective?
- ☐ Have your leaders been trained in coaching and brain-based feedback?
- ☐ Do you have methods for training your employees in receiving coaching and feedback?
- ☐ Do you have a method for measuring the impact of your performance evaluation process?

Summary

It comes back to W. Edwards Deming's approach: Train managers well and do without the performance review process. To assist team members in improving performance, it is essential to ensure that managers see their role as that of coaches and do not "police" performance. Managers need to be trained to coach effectively and use a consistent, easy, and fair model. A manager who can coach an employee to be more successful in his or her current role or to prepare the employee for a future role builds trust. As already noted, trust is a key component for successful review discussions and to prevent the sense of threat that reviews generally engender. Take a look at the process you are using today. Test managers—as well as employees—on how successful they think the process is. You will undoubtedly find that what we have said in this chapter is true just from this simple exercise. Next, examine where you can make changes and most importantly create a culture of coaching. You will be amazed how the dialogue will change over the next two to three years.

CHAPTER SEVEN

LEARNING AND DEVELOPMENT

by Frank Wagner

*T*alent and learning go hand in hand. Your best talent earns this distinction every year because they have the desire and confidence to learn and develop themselves. They do not have to be cajoled into it. They will seek it out on their own if the organization does not provide for this need, even if this means paying for it out of their own pockets and doing it on their own time.

Talent-branding organizations act just like their best talent. They actively provide the learning and development opportunities that performers need to stay on top. In the past, this was accomplished by providing training using skilled facilitators who presented the most up-to-date material from the latest best-selling books. Top talent was honored by special invitation to attend presentations by famous people who talked about leadership.

Similar training recognized the rest of the organization's leadership with workshops led by talented and qualified professionals from inside or outside the company. In larger organizations, the training and development budget was in the millions of dollars. Training was an annual event, or spaced to occur at meaningful transitions in a person's career progression.

That was the past. The present offers a different picture. Technology has provided learning opportunities in a vastly different manner. The ability to involve people from across the globe simultaneously and to break learning into smaller bites that can be experienced with regular frequency has changed the development space. If you have done your homework in the previous chapters you will have a clear and actionable plan for enhancing the needed skills and for closing the developmental gaps. A lot of money is spent on getting the right content to the right recipient. Doing thorough assessments and ensuring alignment to goals and values goes a long way toward mitigating money being spent on the wrong areas. Additionally, it provides the much-needed basis for measuring improvement in workforce quality as a result of targeted development. However, identical to the past, present-day organizations typically do not spend enough time, energy, and budget on follow-up after training. To validate this assertion, do the following exercise.

Exercise 7.1: Your Personal Experience

Look at your personal experience in developing your own talents, and answer the following questions:

1. *How much time (and money) has been spent on your development (include classroom training, distance, and experiential learning)?*

_____

_____

2. *How much time (and money) has been spent in following up on the above to ensure that the investment actually led to new behaviors or habits that helped you apply what you learned?*

_____

_____

Then ask the same question to a half dozen people you know who work in your organization. You can also do this with your neighbors and friends. Does a pattern emerge? We think you will find that follow-up is one area that organizations systematically ignore. There are many reasons for this. It takes time to do and often the initial baseline has not been captured against which to measure improvement and show impact. When follow-up is ignored and organizations run into tough times, often the first thing to get cut is training and development. The reason for this, in part, is that the clear cause-and-effect impact of development cannot be shown. Follow-up with metrics is essential to mitigate this. Another reason for systematic follow-up is that it has been proven that people can change, but without systematic follow-up, they inevitably fall back into old patterns over a period of time.

Providing Learning and Development to Your Talent

In the future, organizations known for talent branding will change where they spend their money. They will pick the right content for their talent to learn, based on their organizational vision, values, strategy, and a thorough talent assessment. In other words, they will focus their initial investment and spend less on what is taught and learned through classroom activity and spend more time on overall learning strategies. This will allow for more investment in follow-up where learning becomes standard practice and part of the organization's "DNA" and brand. Talent-branded organizations will spend more time and energy on follow-up to ensure that learning is transferred to action. The four questions we asked in *Optimizing Talent* are important to answer here:

Exercise 7.2: Ensuring that Learning Is Transferred to Action

1. *How do you determine which learning and development offerings to provide?*

_____

_____

2. *How do you assess the impact of your talent training and development initiatives?*

_____

_____

3. *How do you assure that the lessons and skills learned get utilized back on the job?*

_____

_____

4. *What kind of follow-up do you build into your developmental experience to test learning and validate behavior change?*

_____

_____

Talent-branded organizations will build off of the right set of strengths and change those behaviors that get in the way of helping achieve their strategic focus. They will do this because they clearly understand the development requirements for the future and the capability of their current talent pool, and they have done a systematic and thorough gap analysis to drive action.

A Case Study: Phillips 66

A case example of how this works today is the marketing function for Phillips 66, a large multinational petroleum company. They sourced Prism Ltd. to provide a framework for their top leadership that fit the company's vision, values, and strategy. They planned for and designed the follow-up to this training up front. Internal resources from HR were trained and certified in Stakeholder-Centered Coaching, a methodology based on the principles and practices of world-renowned coach Marshall Goldsmith.

Starting at the top of the organization, three sessions were spaced six months apart during which leaders attended training and new internal coaches certified and paired up with the leaders. Unlike traditional training and development, the training was only the beginning of the learning journey. Following the training, each leader chose a specific leadership development goal and a set of stakeholders who would serve as ongoing sources of feedback and suggestions. This was discussed and agreed upon by each leader's manager.

Each leader partnered with an internal coach with whom they would work over the coming 12 months. Using stakeholders for monthly feedback and suggestions, each leader developed a dynamic action plan to improve in his or her chosen leadership development goal. Senior coaches from Prism Ltd. coached the top two leaders, as well as provided ongoing direction and support to the internal coaches in monthly conference calls. At six-month intervals, each leader was provided an anonymous mini-survey report where all stakeholders rated the level of improvement toward their goals.

After receiving the results of the mini-survey, each leader completed an after-action assessment of his or her progress and what had been learned. This was sent to both manager and to Andy Viens, the company president. This is what Andy Viens said about this process: "Given my years of experience, I was skeptical that training and coaching would have any real impact on the organization. Now that I've been through this process, especially the quality and commitment of follow-up, I am a convert. This stuff works. It is hard work. Yet, I have seen amazing results and now know talent development can, and does, work."

As this case study demonstrates, the key to a talent-branding strategy that provides your talent with genuine growth and development is a process that is heavily loaded for follow-up and support as new skills are learned.

Exercise 7.3: Tell Me a Story.

Assume you are interviewing a candidate for your organization. This person is so talented that getting him or her to join your company would be a real coup. The problem is that this person has already received numerous job offers and getting him or her to pick your organization is a highly competitive endeavor. This person asks you the following question: "What proof do you have that your company believes in investing in the development of its leaders?" What is your best story? What do you say?

Write your story here and analyze it. Is it consistent with your values, mission, and vision? Would potential candidates recognize your story in the reality of the experience they will have when they join your company? If not – refer to Chapters Two, Three, and Four.

_____

_____

_____

_____

_____

_____

_____

_____

_____

_____

What's the Plan?

Planning the learning journey for your talent is best done by starting with the end in mind. What are the key leadership competencies, articulated in concrete actions/behaviors, that can be enhanced or improved upon through an investment in training and development? If you have done your work in Chapters Two, Three, and Four, this should be an easy step.

When developing a plan to connect your learning and development to your talent-branding strategy, consider the following points:

- There are a lot of excellent frameworks for determining what makes a good leader and a good employee. With so many choices, your organization has to edit down what you offer for development. Paring down, editing, and choosing between positive choices is hard to do. Doing this successfully is a matter of constantly implementing a Pareto analysis that answers the question: Is what we are doing contributing to the 20% that adds 80% of value to what our talent needs to learn and practice? This is a constant process, as the environment doesn't stay the same. If the strategy has to change, so will the focus points for your talent development process. Too frequently we see development strategies that are a long list of competencies that no one could accomplish. Whittling your list down to a critical few is hard, but necessary, particularly if you are to measure impact over the long term and you wish to do some analysis that is more predictive of success. (See Chapter Nine.)

- Stick with the basics. Do not fall into the trap of adding new learning from the latest best-selling author until what you have selected for talent development is part of the DNA of the organization. In every profession, top-rated talent is relentless in doing the basics right. Ensure that you have the right measurement tools to verify that you are achieving the development goals that you have set. These measures are based on your talent assessment and people demonstrating over the long-term that the behaviors expected of top talent are being used after they have been learned. One tool that is user-friendly and efficient for measuring behavior change is the mini-survey tool. Similar to a more extensive 360° feedback tool, this tool simply asks less than a handful of question that are customized to what your talent is working to improve.

- Spend more time and dollars on what happens back on the job after training. It is common sense that someone doesn't learn a skill in a few days. Nor does someone learn a new skill by reading or sitting in a classroom. We learn twice: first in our heads and then in our actions. Spend your budget on talent development in the second phase.

The best approach for doing this is a combination of feedback, feedforward (suggestions for the future), and support. (Goldsmith, 2002) The person who can often best provide this is a coach. Over the long haul, the best coaches are the managers, peers, and direct reports of the talent being developed. The next best are internal coaches who have the knowledge and skill to provide this valuable service. In last place is the external coach who helps the immediate situation, not the long-term.

Chapter Seven Checklist

Please review this checklist to see where you and your organization stands on leadership and development.

☐ Are your training strategies aligned to measurable and specific gaps or key future development needs required by the strategic direction of the company?

☐ Has a thorough individual assessment been done?

☐ Is a clear personal action plan in place that can be measured?

☐ Is there a mechanism for follow-up at specified intervals?

☐ Is the follow-up approach systematic and both quantitative and qualitative (bullet points of anecdotal information on improvement is not enough to show impact!)?

☐ Do your learning and development roadmaps employ a wide variety of approaches and more than just classroom based?

If you can answer "yes" to most of these questions, you are ready to move to the next section. If you have gaps, refer to the previous chapters to give you guidance for additional approaches to strengthen your learning about development plans and actions.

Summary

Today there is a lot of money and effort spent on learning and development, but too often not enough rigorous effort to measure a cause-and-effect relationship. This will impact your organization if your brand is perceived as a great place for talent to learn and grow, and also makes learning and development departments vulnerable in times of economic downturn. Without solid, quantified data showing long-term improvement over time, you will struggle to keep the commitment and support of top leadership and you will have great difficulty keeping your workforce sharp and competitive. We discussed this thoroughly in Chapters Three and Four. As we mentioned, there is a symbiotic relationship between the outcomes and improvement of talent through systematic development and the ability to sustain leadership commitment and culture where learning is part of an organization's DNA. Make sure that your learning and development strategies are hardwired to the strategic direction of the organization, that they have concrete baselines and measures to predict future impact, and that they are the basis for more robust predictive analysis to further focus your talent efforts.

CHAPTER EIGHT

HUMAN RESOURCES CAPABILITY

by Liza Sichon

The human resources (HR) function of an organization plays a critical and evolving role in implementing an effective talent management and assessment system. HR professionals are partners with line managers and primarily the ones responsible for designing, assessing, and developing the talent required for the organization today and into the future. While HR is generally aware of this responsibility, most HR functions are understaffed, under-skilled, or over-extended. Individuals have full plates or are not sufficiently trained to manage the demanding talent requirements of their businesses.

For HR to have credibility in the talent arena, they need to be viewed as leaders who demonstrate a direct link from talent investment to business success. They also need to be viewed as role models for optimizing talent within their own function and throughout the company. The five evolving roles that HR leaders of the future need to master are:

1. Chief Cultural Officer and Cultural Promoter

Culture is organic, not static. The danger of keeping or preserving culture is the tendency to make it stale or inflexible. Instead, HR leaders need to promote the desired culture of the organization consistent with changing business requirements and aspirational values. However, do not confuse promoting the culture with keeping the culture. HR has the unique role of ensuring that organization leaders role model and are accountable for the values and culture. There is nothing worse than having ever-changing values and leaders who don't live up to the expectations for leadership behavior that these values imply. When leader behaviors do not reflect the organization's values, cynicism sets in, and this cynicism erodes the talent brand. HR professionals must hold up the mirror to the organization and help move the culture in an aspirational direction. They need to be skilled at helping the organization's leaders navigate this very important and often invisible aspect of the organization. Chapter Three and Four of this workbook go into great detail on ways you can ensure cultural alignment. Refer back to these chapters for guidance on specific steps you can take to build a strong culture that supports a talent brand.

2. Executive and Team Coach

While we do not discount the critical value of one-on-one executive coaching, the HR leader needs to be able to effectively coach teams as well. Often the interplay between the leader and her team is an essential dynamic that needs to be addressed. Coaching the leader in consort with her team has proven to be a powerful tool in building the open communication, trust, and collaboration that is essential for any leadership team's success. If the leader and her team do not reflect the values and act accordingly, the culture will stay static. Research from *Optimizing Talent* (Sharkey and Eccher, 2010) shows that a culture that remains passive or aggressive and loses sight of a constructive high-performance culture ultimately loses market value and talent.

3. Talent Assessor

People are the core of every organization's success and having the right people at the right time doing the right thing brings about organizational success. Chapter Five goes into great detail on how to assess talent. HR professionals should be highly trained in this core skill and coach their business partners to effectively assess talent. The second a person is promoted who does not reflect the stated values and behaviors required, a message is sent to everyone in the organization that culture and values are not important. This will have a reverberating effect on the organization.

4. Organizational Strategist

Given the numerous models in the marketplace, it is important that the HR professionals have tried and tested models for major organizational processes. They must have organization development capabilities and be able to clearly diagnosis complex organization issues for the root causes and design concrete methods to effectively address them. The absence of tested models means the HR professional must invent them on the fly, resulting in unpredictable outcomes. HR professionals need to be as skilled in team building, driving organizational change, assessing culture, and creating effective strategic alignment as they are in compensation, labor relations, and other aspects of HR. In fact, we would argue that as the world gets more complex, technology becomes more pervasive, and business more global, these strategies will become increasingly important. The classic HR work will become more digital, thus requiring a new and more sophisticated set of tools.

5. Talent Analyst and Insight Provider

More and more companies today use data to analyze their workforce. Obtaining data is not enough. Understanding the correlation of multiple data points and using this data to make the business successful is the key strategy that every HR professional needs to understand. Converting data to knowledge and knowledge to insight is a critical role of the HR professional. Sharkey and Eccher (2010) point out that most HR professionals spend the majority of their time on data analytic systems, while not enough time is spent on the insights these systems can provide. Bersin (2013) showed that little has changed on the maturity of HR to provide deep insight into predictive trends that help organizations drive greater talent focus and alignment to business outcomes. Chapter Nine goes into detail about how you can sharpen this skill.

Exercise 8.1: The HR Talent Capability Assessment

Take the assessment below to determine your own capabilities and that of your team. For every statement, rate yourself on a scale from 1(lowest) to 10 (highest).

1. Cultural Promoter

_____ a. I am clear about the culture that my organization wants to promote.

_____ b. I have a clearly defined process to regularly assess our culture.

_____ c. My business leaders buy into the cultural transformation that we need to undertake to meet our long-term business objectives.

_____ d. For each milestone of the cultural transformation, we have clearly defined "action steps" we need to take.

_____ e. I know exactly where we are blocked or when we stop taking action due to fear or frustration.

_____ = *Total*

2. Executive and Team Coach

_____ a. I have the certification, training, and skills needed to be an executive coach.

_____ b. I have established credibility to coach my business leaders and the team.

_____ c. I have my own coach who stretches me to achieve my own goals.

_____ d. I ask thought-provoking questions and I actively listen. I don't tell people what to do.

_____ e. I have a coaching contract with my clients that includes coaching goals with clear, quantifiable measures for success.

_____ = *Total*

3. Talent Assessor

_____ a. I understand the skills, behaviors, and motivations that determine success for each role.

_____ b. I have a consistent, proven, and reliable set of tools to assess talent.

_____ c. I regularly receive feedback and training on my own assessment skills and expertise.

_____ d. I have a clear and articulated talent assessment strategy, including tracking of decisions made on selection, promotions, and succession planning.

_____ = *Total*

4. Organizational Strategist

_____ a. I know how to assess and diagnose an organizational problem, large or small.

_____ b. I have a set of proven models to drive change.

_____ c. I have a clear communication strategy that supports the change process.

_____ d. I understand and apply the appropriate motivations and rewards associated with bringing people along.

_____ e. I can correlate organizational actions with business strategies and can quantify the results.

_____ = *Total*

5. Analyst and Insight Provider

_____ a. I use multiple methods to collect and convert talent data to useful information.

_____ b. Talent insight influences our people practices: selection and promotion.

_____ c. Talent and culture reports are discussed by business leaders on a regular basis similar to financial results.

_____ d. Based on talent analytics, I know the profile of teams or individuals who can be successful today and in the future of our company.

_____ e. Our desired leadership behaviors are linked to high performance outcomes and business results.

_____ = *Total*

Exercise 8.2: Action Planning

Once you have taken the assessment, answer the following questions:

1. What are your top three strengths?

a. _____

b. _____

c. _____

2. What are your top three areas of improvement? These do not mean lowest scores, but can also be your top three choices where you want to be better.

a. _____

b. _____

c. _____

3. *What actions can you take to close the gaps in your profile? Who will you share this with and by when will you complete this?*

a. _____

b. _____

c. _____

Exercise 8.3: Hiring for Success Interview Guide

If you are hiring a top-notch HR leader, below are some interview questions you can ask to ensure that you are bringing in a professional with the potential or experience in five critical HR roles. Feel free to add your own questions to this list.

Cultural Promoter Questions

1. *Name an experience where you were in a successful culture. What were its attributes and what did you do to promote or preserve this culture?*

2. *Describe the worst environment that you have been in. What happened and what did you do about it?*

3. *What are some of the cultural levers that you have used that worked? What didn't work? What were the results? How would you use them differently?*

4. _____

5. _____

Executive and Team Coach Questions

1. *How do you listen? What do you listen for when you coach others?*

2. *Give me an example of your most difficult coaching client. What did you do? What happened? How did you work together?*

3. *What are some of the most effective ways you have coached leadership teams? How did you measure success?*

4. _____

5. _____

Talent Assessor Questions

1. *Cite an example of a hiring mistake. What happened? What did you do?*

2. *When is someone ready for promotion? What are the critical attributes a person needs to be promoted? Which skills can be learned or developed, and how? Which skills cannot be learned or developed?*

3. *What does it mean to be a "high potential"? Is this learned or developed? How? How can your organization build a strong talent pool of ready successors?*

4. *What are some of the most effective ways to quickly assess talent in an acquisition scenario where you have ten days or less to make a decision on the top team?*

5. _____

Organizational Strategist Questions

1. *What methodology do you use to diagnose and assess an organization?*

2. *What has worked for you and what hasn't? How did you fix it?*

3. *How do you communicate bad news to an organization?*

4. *What systems and rewards structure have you put in place to promote desired change?*

5. _____

Talent Analyst Questions

1. *What various data have you used to assess talent in your organization?*

2. *How did you introduce or lead a data-based talent discussion with your business leaders? What did you learn? What would you do differently?*

3. *How do you know when it is time to change what you are measuring?*

4. *What have you done to introduce talent analytics to your team? How did you teach your HR team to be knowledgeable in talent analytics?*

5. _____

Exercise 8.4: Case Study

Company XYZ was faced with competitive and business turnaround challenges. Revenue and profits were not improving enough. They knew that to win in this market they needed the best people in their industry. They wanted to ensure that they were able to attract top external talent while developing their own internal talent. The CEO believed that leadership was a critical element to the future success of the company.

There was no consistent language or process for defining talent, nor was there a system wide framework to identify, develop, and promote the best talent. Talent identification and development were dependent on local leaders. The CEO was not able to consistently view the caliber of talent across the company.

The internal talent management group was tasked to design a talent assessment process to determine the quality of leadership and to gain a benchmark process as to the developmental needs of its leaders. As part of this initiative a leadership framework was established. This framework was developed with an eye towards the leadership behavioral requirements of the future. The framework was rigorously validated with a wide spectrum of internal functional and business leaders to ensure it reflected a consensus of the desired future state.

With this foundation, the talent group crafted an assessment strategy to achieve an objective and unbiased assessment of the top leadership talent of the company. The purpose of the assessment was the following:

- Gain a clear picture of the strengths of leadership talent across the organization at the enterprise, team, or functional levels, and at the individual levels.

- Understand the leadership gaps that needed to be filled through a variety of strategies such as coaching, development, rotational assignments, etc.

- Provide feedback coaching and action planning support to each of the executives involved in the process.

- Support the business and functional leads in developing a talent strategy to continue to develop their teams.

After much discussion with the business leaders, it was clear that for development purposes, the project would increase the executive strength of the company. All communications were designed to communicate these messages.

To address the need for an unbiased view, a third-party assessment team comprised of industrial and organizational psychologists/consultants was hired. To compliment the internal HR team, the external consultants had a joint planning session to design the overall project plan, the assessment approach, the behavioral anchors to be used to assess talent, and the interview guide and protocol to ensure there was consistency in the methodology. Every assessor was trained in this approach. The materials and the approach were reviewed with the leadership team, as were the measures that were to be used as the benchmarks. A robust communication plan was put in place so that all participants became familiar with the process, the assessors, and the developmental reports.

The assessment process consisted of the following:

- An individual one-hour interview, during which participants used the agreed to questions and guide

- A one-hour interview with the participants' bosses to gain their views

- An additional five interviews with peers, subordinates, or key stakeholders that were agreed upon with the participants, their bosses, and their HR leaders

An individual report was generated based upon the findings. Each participant received a personal copy of his or her report along with a development plan. The participants also took part in a one- or two-hour personal debrief with their assessor/coach, so that they thoroughly understood the data. During this discussion, the coach worked with the participants to help them create a development plan. Participants were encouraged to share their plans with their bosses, although it was not a requirement. Aggregate reports were shared with the business and functional leaders of the groups that reported to them. An overall picture was provided to the leadership along with strategies to close the gaps. Partnerships were created with the training team to assist them in developing leadership programs focused on the key development areas. Talent was eventually ranked as top, middle, or bottom talent.

In parallel, the HR team underwent special training to help them learn how to effectively assess talent, provide constructive feedback, and help coach talent for improvement. The plan was to begin to build the skill set internally into the company HR environment. In this way, they would be self-sufficient and able to carry on the assessment and more specifically the developmental coaching conversations.

The regional and business HR leaders were engaged to implement and support the plan. As expected, there was skepticism and fear about the process, but since this was a leadership mandate, the HR team had to support the plan.

As the program gained traction as an executive development process, there was interest in taking it deeper into the organization through the vice presidential ranks and ultimately to the directors. At this juncture, because of changes in priorities and a focus on cost, scalability, and speed, the process evolved. The process was used as an input to exit low performers. The assessments ultimately were reduced to about an hour in length with limited cross reference checks with others.

The third party categorized talent as top, mid, and bottom talent. This information was not shared broadly, but was included in confidential talent profiles, talent discussions with senior leaders, and promotional decisions.

Over time, the majority of the bottom classified talent left the company and some top talent was promoted or left for larger roles. Some of the mid talent people stayed as they were, some of them were promoted and some eventually left the company.

1. What did this company do right?

a. _____

_____

_____

b. _____

_____

_____

c. _____

_____

_____

2. What can this company improve or do differently?

a. _____

_____

_____

b. _____

_____

_____

c. _____

_____

_____

3. *If you were to implement a talent assessment strategy in your company, how would you do it?*

a. _____

_____

_____

b. _____

_____

_____

4. *How valid is the use of external assessors? How can external talent assessors be used effectively to assess talent objectively?*

a. _____

_____

_____

b. _____

_____

_____

5. *How could the talent management group collaborate effectively with the human resources leaders who were tasked with implementation to make this process sustainable and effective?*

a. _____

_____

_____

b. _____

_____

_____

6. *Do you agree with categorizing talent: Top, Middle and Bottom? What are the benefits and risks of labeling talent. What would you do differently?*

a. _____

_____

_____

b. _____

_____

_____

7. *How would you get the buy in of the leaders who are being assessed? How is it possible to position and communicate this differently with the managers and leaders?*

a. _____

_____

_____

b. _____

_____

_____

Chapter Eight Checklist

Before moving on to Chapter Nine, we recommend that you review this checklist. If you can answer in the affirmative to most of these questions, then you are ready to move on.

☐ Have you assessed yourself relative to the above questions?

☐ Have you assessed your team for its capabilities?

☐ Have you validated you assessment of yourself and your team with other key stakeholders in the organization?

☐ Do you have an honest picture of your team's capability that you can take action on?

☐ Have you shared the results with your team, including your personal results?

☐ Have you created clear development goals for the team?

☐ Do you have a specific action plan in place to close any gaps?

☐ Have you defined how you will measure and track progress?

Summary

The role of HR in talent-optimized organizations remains critical. For HR leaders to be credible, they need to be role models of talent best practices within their HR functions, continuously improve their skills and capabilities in the five HR roles, and align talent practices with business strategies and goals. Whether you lead a global HR function or an HR unit, you must consider yourself a business leader and do what all business leaders do. Develop a vision for your function aligned to the organization goals, create a clear strategy for HR to move the function forward, measure your impact regularly, and adjust as appropriate. If you do this, your function will never get stale or obsolete, but only increase in its importance and impact.

CHAPTER NINE

DATA ANALYTICS

by Linda D. Sharkey PhD

Data analytics can be daunting at best for most organizations and for human resource (HR) professionals. The reason usually lies with the following issues:

1. *Having the data in the first place*

2. *The quality of the data that you do have*

3. *The ability to integrate the data sources to that they are usable and tell a story*

4. *Using systems that collect the data in efficient and effective ways – moving beyond the spreadsheets*

5. *Finding human resource professionals who are facile with statistics and analytics*

We found in our initial research for *Optimizing Talent* (Sharkey and Eccher, 2010) that most HR professionals were spending the majority of their time installing technology systems like Saba, People Soft, Oracle, or other products to collect the data that they would ultimately need. This in itself is not bad. In fact, it is an important first step in many cases. However, much more work needs to be done to make these systems usable for predictive and analytical purposes. We equate the state of data analytics to my early experience with companies trying to implement Six Sigma. The foundation of Six Sigma initiatives has two important elements:

1. *Having the right questions that will be answered through analysis, and*

2. *Having the necessary data to effectively answer those questions.*

Like Six Sigma, the fundamentals need to be put in place in order for data analytics to be a true business lever for change and insight. Recent research by Bersin by Deloitte (2013) looked further into the issue of data analytics and found that 86% of the organizations they surveyed focused primarily on reporting. Bersin also pointed out that the data are often driven by compliance issues or ad hoc requests that are reactive rather than proactive (Bersin, et al. 2013). Unfortunately, these findings indicate that the field has not progressed as far as I would have hoped since Paul Eccher and I did our research for *Optimizing Talent*. However, we do see a greater emphasis being placed on the need for talent data analytics and increased rigor through the discipline of strategic workforce planning. For me, strategic workforce planning is an integral part of any robust talent planning model. It is the predictive analytics that is needed to support strong talent decisions aligned to business results.

At Hewlett Packard, the early leader and pacesetter in the field of workforce planning, we tied talent management closely to strategic workforce planning. As a result, we were able to make some early and strong predictive moves for business success. We were able to predict staffing patterns for emerging markets and determine talent quality that would drive business outcomes. Both elements provided compelling insights for talent decision-making purposes.

However, this discipline continues to need to mature. The Bersin research provides a good operating model for diagnosing where you and your organization stand in your journey to predictive analytics – the ultimate goal.

FIG 9.1: BERSIN BY DELOITTE
TALENT ANALYTICS MATURITY MODEL

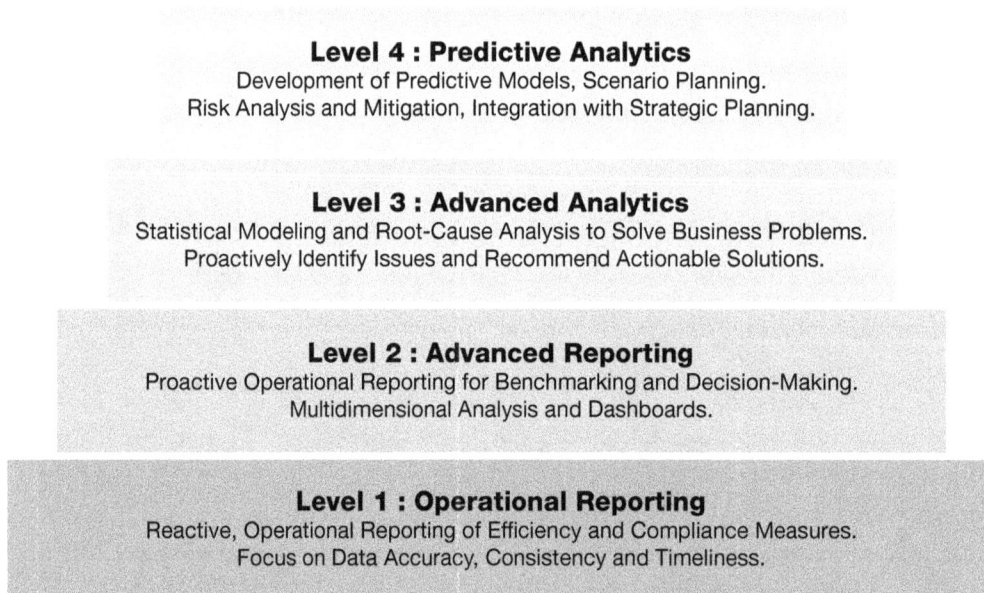

Level 4 : Predictive Analytics
Development of Predictive Models, Scenario Planning.
Risk Analysis and Mitigation, Integration with Strategic Planning.

Level 3 : Advanced Analytics
Statistical Modeling and Root-Cause Analysis to Solve Business Problems.
Proactively Identify Issues and Recommend Actionable Solutions.

Level 2 : Advanced Reporting
Proactive Operational Reporting for Benchmarking and Decision-Making.
Multidimensional Analysis and Dashboards.

Level 1 : Operational Reporting
Reactive, Operational Reporting of Efficiency and Compliance Measures.
Focus on Data Accuracy, Consistency and Timeliness.

Source: Bersin by Deloitte, 2013

From the research, we know that only 4% of the companies studied reached the most mature phase of talent data analytics, which is *predictive analytics*. (For our purposes here, *predictive analytics* are defined as the ability to forecast future talent outcomes.) The majority of the companies indicated that they were still at Level 1, as the model shows, reporting only data on efficiency and compliance measures. As you can see, there is work to be done in this area in order to gain the insights to fully optimize your workforce.

Steps to Get You Started on the Analytics Journey

Let's go back to Chapters Three and Four in this workbook. Ask yourself: What are the critical issues that are most important for your leadership relative to their strategy and being able to predict workforce top performance? By now, you should have a clear indication of the talent issues that need to be solved for your organization. For instance, what types of talent will be most successful in the organization? How quickly will certain individuals be able to add value? What cultural elements are most strongly aligned to business success? Which individuals will do best in global assignments? Who has the best aptitude for sales roles?

These questions should go far beyond the standard question of who will be retiring in the next five years. For instance, who are the best successors for those who will leave their roles in the next five years? How deep is the talent pipeline? How many people do you have in top talent roles? Who is willing to move, is ready for, or wants a global role? These questions are important because they 1) focus on the future, and 2) elevate your thinking to a higher level on the maturity curve. As a result, your data analysis will provide more compelling, actionable, and predictive insights.

Here are the steps you need to take to create a world-class workforce.

Exercise 9.1: Steps to a World-Class Workforce

Step 1: Maturity Curve Analysis

Decide where you are the on the Bersin by Deloitte Talent Analytics Maturity Model. Where would you place your organization on this maturity curve and why? Based upon this placement, determine three actions you can take to move to the next level.

1. _____

2. _____

3. _____

Step 2: Operating Hypothesis Crystallization

What are the key questions you are trying to solve? Based upon your previous analyses in this workbook, what is the most compelling workforce question that needs to be answered? What is your and your leader's hypothesis about the most compelling question(s)? A great deal of time and energy will go into answering these questions, so getting the right question(s) is key. Write down the questions. Do some external benchmarking and environmental scanning. What have others done about these questions, if anything, and what are some of the issues in the environment that might impact the study of this hypothesis (e.g., demographics, political issues, etc.) Check out the book *Strategic Workforce Planning* by Tracey Smith (2012) for further insight into these topics.

Questions to answer:

1. _____

2. _____

3. _____

Next, test the key questions with your leaders or business partners. Validate that they are important and test their operating hypothesis. Then, finalize your research questions and move onto the
next step.

Final questions:

1. _____

2. _____

3. _____

Step 3: *Current Data Available*

What current data do you have to answer these questions? What do you know today about your
workforce? What insights do your data give you about your current state? Are there any correlations
that can be made from what you already know? For example, how has your top talent performed in
global assignments? What leadership behaviors did they consistently exhibit?

List everything you currently know:

1. _____

2. _____

3. _____

What does it tell you?

1. _____

2. _____

3. _____

Step 4: *Data Gaps*

What don't you know that you need to know in order to answer your key questions and support or
disprove your hypothesis? Make a list of the key gaps. Remember that you can over- collect data, and
this is costly. Narrow your data needs to the most important factors or variables. A word of caution:
if you have a question about a data element, you should probably collect the information up front,
as it is very difficult and time-consuming to go back and collect additional data after the fact. This is
a crucial step that requires a good degree of thought. Deciding on the key variables that will impact

your question is also very important. For example, is the quality of the manager or a top global talent important to the equation, or is time in the role more important? I would recommend that you test the gaps and variables with your business partners and other human resource professionals to ensure that you have not missed important data elements.

List the data that you think you will need:

1. _____

2. _____

3. _____

What are some variables that will be essential to solving the question(s) at hand?

1. _____

2. _____

3. _____

Step 5: Data Collection Methodology

Decide on your data collection methodology. What platform will you use to capture the data? Here is an area where you can get tripped up. You may not have the technological systems to capture the data. This is often the case. Because of this factor alone, HR has often been forced into the box of selecting the technology platform as its first step. This can and is extremely time-consuming and can keep HR from doing more sophisticated work. If you find yourself in this situation, don't abandon the installation of the technology platform, but don't stop your data collection project either. Do the project on a pilot scale and use old-fashioned data collection methods to get the baseline you need to do the correlations and analysis. There are very sophisticated programs out today that make this step easy. The most important thing is to have a solid design for how you will collect your data. We often recommend that you consult Six Sigma or ask Six Sigma talent in the organization for help. Perhaps you might employ outside help to ensure you get what you need and want for this step. For those of you who have done this type of research before, you know how important it is to have a well-conceived data collection method.

Define the steps of your data collection approach here:

1. _____

2. _____

3. _____

Step 6: Data Analysis

Here is where you will use cause-and-effect analysis. Analysis programs exist on the internet today in much easier forms then they did even three years ago. You can literally drop your spreadsheets into these programs and run the analysis. Consult for assistance. Factor analysis is always a good start. Seeing which variable or elements cluster or factor with each other is at the heart of data analysis.

List how you will analyze the data using a program that relates to the question(s) you are attempting to answer.

1. _____

2. _____

3. _____

Step 7: *Define the Study Results*

What did you learn? What answers did you get for your key questions? Now you can begin to answer the questions upon which you started your study. This is a micro-view of the study and the impact it has had.

Write the key insights:

1. _____

2. _____

3. _____

Step 8: *Define the Impact Results*

This is an important, yet different, step in thinking about and analyzing the results of your data analysis. Did what you learn impact business outcomes in any way? For example, did retention improve as a result of your study? What about costs of hiring, recruitment, etc.? This is a great place to look at the Bersin by Deloitte Talent Analytics Maturity Model for measuring impact. (See Figure 9.1.)

The Bersin Model dovetails with the results and business outcomes highlighted in the research Paul Eccher and I did for *Optimizing Talent* (2010). If you have these types of business outcomes and results to report on the macro level, you should do so. Keep this step in mind, because it is the essential element for why these types of initiative are so important to company or organization success, whether you are a publically traded, private nonprofit, public sector, or private company.

What has the business impact been for your project?

1. _____

2. _____

3. _____

What had you expected the impact to be?

1. _____

2. _____

3. _____

Step 9: _Strategic Redefinition_

Create the strategy to close the gaps. This is an important step and requires that you go back to the beginning of the Optimizing Talent model. It is particularly important to look at the operating section of the model in order to refine approaches. What needs to change as a result of the data you found? Do you have to change any of your approaches to talent to reflect the new findings? Does your assessment model need to be refined? Is your performance system capturing what you need? Does your development approach need adjusting? Does your recruitment strategy need to change, as well as how you onboard and develop talent? Are your criteria for selecting successors still valid or do they need to be adjusted?

These are just some of the questions you should consider in refining your strategy for the coming year. Remember that, as you revise your strategy, you also need to revise your data collection approach and create a new baseline for measurement of your revised strategies' impact. It is important to be thinking about potential business impact measures. How has what you have done impacted your business?

My new strategy is:

1. _____

2. _____

3. _____

The elements of the model I need to adjust are:

1. _____

2. _____

3. _____

The primary adjustments will be:

1. _____

2. _____

3. _____

Additional data collection needs, if appropriate:

1. _____

2. _____

3. _____

Step 10: _Communicating Results_

A key element of this step is to create the story for the rest of the organization, in particular, your leadership team and business partner. What does the study suggest and what is your recommendation for closing the gaps? You will also need to define how best to communicate your revised strategy to the rest of the organization. In this step, it is essential that you determine the best spokesperson to share the results and any strategic changes that will impact the workforce. Consideration should also be given to the communication medium for delivering the changes.

The key messages to be communicated are:

1. _____

2. _____

3. _____

How will they be communicated and by when?

1. _____

2. _____

3. _____

Who will be doing the communication?

1. _____

2. _____

3. _____

Words of Caution

After many years of doing data collection, analysis, and trying to drive data-driven decision making relative to human capital issues, I have learned a number of things that I want to share with you. First, beware the tyranny of averages. Averages can hide a multitude of sins. Let me cite this real case study.

The diversity team at a major technology company was reporting numbers on female-diverse hires and promotions. They had set a percent increase target for women in the workforce worldwide. Year after year, they touted their success at increasing women in the workforce and gained high accolades for doing so. However, when one dug deeper into the data, it was found that the increase in women in the workforce was actually due to hiring or promoting at administrative levels, not at more senior levels in the organization. In fact, the company was losing women in the higher ranks at an alarming rate. Thus, as you can see, an aggregate percentage can hide a number of egregious problems and flaws.

This case study points out two other cautions: 1) making the data pool too broad, and 2) not having a clearly enough defined goal. Let me elaborate. When the data pool is too broad, you lose regional and cultural nuances. In our case study, the hiring of women was going on at a rapid rate in some parts of the world, but the jobs were lower ranking in stature. Obviously, this fact made for a rosier picture than really existed. In addition, the goal statement was flawed. There was a need for two distinct goals:

1) How was the company doing at hiring women by region? and

2) How was it doing at promoting and retaining women at different levels?

Once this was understood and the data was further analyzed, a new strategy was put into place. Specifically, the company focused on the European population of women. They defined who top talent was and who was ready for promotion. They also put in place a rigorous internal promotion process. The results of these actions were impressive. Over an 18-month period, the European region increased the number of women in more senior roles by 36 percent. This case study underscores the power of data analytics in decision making and changing the business impact for an organization. This company became a magnet for talented engineering women all over the region, because the word got out that, as a woman, you could build a career with this company.

This is a perfect example of how developing a strong internal talent brand can create a strong external market brand with limited effort on the part of the company except for understanding the facts and changing their approach. The word got out in the marketplace through word of mouth and of course marketing.

Chapter Nine Checklist

Here is a checklist that you should consider after you have thought through the steps in this chapter.

☐ Do you have a clear hypothesis that everyone can understand?

- Have you tested it with others?

- Is it important to the leadership?

- Is it rooted in the business strategy?

☐ Do you know what data you have relative to the question at hand?

☐ Have you defined the new data you need to collect?

- Have you done an environmental scan to see what data are out there that can inform your question?

- Have you done some scenario planning to clarify possibilities and help you define the variables that will be important to your question or hypothesis?

☐ Did you define a data collection methodology?

- Do you know what business issues you may want to be correlating your data with?

☐ Did you get sign-off on your plan from your key stakeholders?

If you can answer "yes" to most of these, you are ready to go.

Summary

This is probably the most challenging area of the Talent Optimization Framework™. We highlighted this as an emerging and important skillset in the Human Resource Capability chapter, not because it is hard to do once you get the hang of it, but because it is the least-informed area and the area in which HR professionals are currently doing the least amount of work. This will be a growing area of expertise for anyone in the talent space. With the advent of "big data," it is likely to become more important to people and talent decisions as we put more rigors into the process. Use this as an opportunity to hone your skills and practice applying science to your discipline. These skills can assist you in definitively showing a link to real business outcomes. What better way to get a seat at the table and keep it? You will be indispensable!

CHAPTER TEN

APPLYING THE TALENT OPTIMIZATION FRAMEWORK™ CASE STUDIES

by Eve Emerson

Now that you are grounded in the Talent Optimization Framework™, it's time to see how you would apply it to your current situation. How, or does, optimizing talent differ in a large mature organization versus in a smaller organization? In the following case studies, you will see the importance of alignment of all elements of the model to organizational success.

If you are currently in a large organization and want to learn how to implement a successful talent process, read Case #1. This case study describes how a large global information technology organization with over 300,000 employees used the Talent Optimization Framework™. If a small-sized organization reflects your current experience, then please read Case # 2. We were not surprised to see how even a small software company with 5,000 employees managed to optimize talent globally utilizing the same concepts. Regardless of your organization's size, the same systemic approach and components are needed to build an effective talent management system.

Case #1 - Large Global Information Technology Organization (300,000+ employees)

Background

This well-established, global company had over 300,000 employees located in more than 170 countries around the world. It was thrown into turmoil due to market changes and customer demands, which the organization was not prepared to handle. Leaders were focused on individual products, while their customers were looking for broader solutions. The company's annual net losses were in mass proportions and streamlining and cost management were big concerns. During this time, the organization was on the brink of collapse and leaders considered splitting its divisions into separate independent businesses. Before these drastic measures were taken, a new CEO was brought in to try to turn the organization around. This was the first time in the history of the organization an external leader was brought in, and he had to act quickly in order to keep the company whole. Upon arriving, he made dramatic decisions to stabilize the organization, which included rebuilding the product line, shrinking the workforce, and implementing significant cost reductions. The "street" kept asking for his strategy and all he could think about was to stop the bleeding first, then talk strategy. He put in place a completely new leadership team to help drive this turnaround. The team looked at the key elements of the organization and decided that they needed a new approach to talent that would focus on the strategic turnaround. A clear mandate was put forward to build a top leadership team as the key change agent in driving the turnaround.

To keep the organization whole and enable a new leadership team to support that mandate, the organization created a small group of leadership consultants who would support the senior leaders in the execution of their strategy to help the organization regain market leadership as one intact company. The CEO sponsored this group of HR professionals to ensure a focus on building organizational capability (strong leaders and talent pool). They used a multipronged approach for linking business strategy, organizational design, and leadership capability across the leadership teams. The leadership consultants were in the trenches with the senior leaders teaching them how to change leadership skills in real-world situations. The organization believed that the leaders and talent needed to mirror the strategy of the business and that's how this new team designed its approach. The strategy was to be rolled out in phases, moving from a collapsing organization to a turnaround and finally to a transformed high-performing organization that could beat the competition and regain market leadership. What follows is a discussion of what we did at each of the three phases to meet the CEO's objectives.

Phase 1: _Coming Back from Collapse_

When the CEO hired the key HR leader to build the team, his mandate was to focus on his top 300 and "send them back to school." He wanted to ensure that, at the end of the day, we were building a talent pool to become successors and improve the overall organizational capability as well as improve our diversity representation of senior leaders.

To start, the organization created key leadership competencies as the foundation for the effort (and making their value proposition of owning the market where business problems intersected with technology. These competencies were used for the sole purpose of development and were embedded in talent reviews and all leadership programs. Each business leader had a yearly review with the CEO as well as monthly talent reviews with their direct report teams and peers.

The organization had dedicated talent leaders for each business unit who focused on the talent review process and succession planning. Another group of HR professionals/executive coaches were dedicated to creating strategic learning programs to align to the strategy, as well as serving as consultants to support senior leaders in developing their own leadership competencies and executing their business strategies. The key enablers were in place with senior leadership supporting the process, a critical element of the Talent Optimization Framework™.

We looked at metrics to see how long it took high-potential managers to become executives and how many high-potential executives were promoted to the top 300. There were varying programs to support the acceleration of promotions, such as development centers for high-potential managers soon to be executives and for high-potential executives soon to be nominated to the top 300; there were also 1:1 coaching opportunities. During the first few years of implementation, there were still many "back door" deals going on as leaders were learning to be more methodic, data driven, and transparent about their talent management practices and decisions. Leaders were most comfortable moving the "known talent" and by the third or fourth year, the discussions included a broader spectrum of talent and the leaders were following a more rigorous process.

Phase 2: Turnaround

The turnaround phase focused on how this company would get its second chance at market leadership. The emphasis was on how to increasingly integrate across markets, customers, and product lines in an environment where technology was changing the rules of the marketplace at unprecedented rates. This was an organization that was also shifting from a multinational to a global focus. In order to transform the company, this select HR team drove a consistent leadership development strategy. Their specific focus was on what was happening in the business, leadership challenges for execution, and the experiences that prepared people to meet these challenges. The team embarked on the following key actions and initiatives that were considered forward-thinking approaches:

- Provided coaching on personal leadership and change management based on a core leadership framework

- Advised on organizational design/structure

- Created a homegrown succession management tool to support the process

- Became the corporate center of excellence for competency modeling, coaching, experienced-based development models and development centers

Their support to the business was to ensure that talent became part of the culture of the organization, where every leader was transparent in identifying his or her talent as well as assessing and being proactive in having them available for opportunities around the globe. We were striving for our leaders to demonstrate transparency in their conversations with each other, practicing "straight talk" by telling it like it was. For example, when they talked about moving talent, it needed to be for the development of the individual and the need of the business rather than moving a problem to another part of the business. It wasn't always that way though. The overall command-and-control culture still drove some of the "back door" behavior and leaders were not having the tough conversations. We were striving for a more collaborative culture and our new processes clearly supported that, though it took many years to become part of the fabric of the organization.

Phase 3: High-Performing Organization

What did the organization need to do to shift from a turnaround to a high-performing organization? Approximately six years into this strategy, the organization needed to transform how it was viewed in the market; its primary focus was to integrate itself in front of the clients. The rate and pace of change in the information technology industry continues to accelerate, so the organization now had to "up its game" to change its culture through leadership. With the core processes in place, it was easier to focus on the leadership mandate, which was to achieve cultural transformation from a command-and-control, internally focused mindset to a more external, marketplace focused culture where leaders could orchestrate change and enable others to act. We needed our leaders to:

- Model collaborative leadership

- Drive integration

- Lead by the company's values

- Create interdependence and become more integrated with each other

- Be accountable for the enterprise agenda

The leadership was pushed even harder to model collective leadership with greater focus on the development of their talent. We made sure that our most senior leaders were also getting involved and sponsoring all of the leadership programs.

We got to a point in the journey where our leaders were comfortable speaking about the core leadership competencies, receiving feedback about their own behaviors, and were openly willing to create more high-performing teams. Leaders were aware of the core development experiences and programs available to them and their teams. They were also open to the leadership and organizational assessments and the coaching that went along with the feedback. The organization also conducted a leadership model update to determine if the leadership competencies first identified were still relevant or had evolved over time. We selected 30 senior leaders who were role models, conducted in-depth behavioral event interviews, collected leadership data, and had the quantitative and qualitative data analyzed by an outside firm. We did find that our compass for leadership shifted from an internal to an external orientation. In addition, leaders demonstrated mutual respect for and trust in colleagues, modeled the company values, and extended their leadership beyond their direct teams to across the entire organization.

The succession-planning process had a clear rhythm that all the business leaders followed. Each leader had an annual review with the CEO of the organization and executive capability. There was also a section at each Operating Council meeting (CEO and direct reports) to recap senior-level moves, review open positions, and discuss high potentials ready for new assignments. All open positions for the top leadership team were vetted and agreed to collectively with the CEO and his direct reports. Then through periodic talent reviews with their teams they were able to gain a consistent view of all open global roles. The leaders were working more collaboratively and there was more opportunity to bring diverse leaders together to solve key business issues.

Exercise 10.1: Moving to the High-Performance Phase

1. If you were the talent leader for this group of HR professionals, what would you do now to move into the transformational high-performing phase of this strategy?

_____

_____

_____

2. Describe how the elements of the Talent Optimization Framework™ were utilized to support the culture and leadership focus areas so far:

a. What worked well?

_____

_____

b. What are a few things they would need to do differently?

_____

_____

c. What does the organization need to focus on now in order to shift into the transformation space?

_____

_____

Case #2 – Small Global Software Organization (5,000 employees)

Background

This global software company has specialized in providing software solutions for the financial services industry over the last 30 years. They are a market leader in banking and treasury and capital markets, serving over 1,800 customers in 120 countries with 5,000 employees. They have received many awards and recognition from leading industry leaders and publications throughout the years. Their customers include some of the world's leading global financial institutions (47 of the world's 50 largest banks). Their business tends to ebb and flow with the changing landscape of the financial markets, with the challenges of deregulation in the 1970s, automated transaction settlement and processing in the 1980s, and ongoing regulatory requirements.

Given the rate and pace of change in the financial markets, the only way to meet customer needs quickly and not start from a blank sheet was through acquisitions. This organization, therefore, focused their strategy on acquisitions to ensure they were always ready for customers with new business or technology challenges. They wanted to be in a position to provide proven quality solutions rather than invent and test. In the company's 30-year history, its growth was predominantly a result of multiple acquisitions of product lines and it operated like a holding company. The culture was such that employees identified themselves with the product, not the name of the overall company. Training happened for each product line and very little was done as one organization—it was a siloed mentality. The company did experience growth in each product line, but it realized that it could get even more. The organization also grew by putting in place a services business that helped to direct its focus to more of a solutions space, which meant that it had to look at the talent.

The organization has been on quite a journey, starting as an independent company, then a public one, at which point a CEO was hired to take it through a turnaround. Most recently, it was acquired by an equity partner and deleted from the London Stock Exchange. This case study will focus on how the organization approached its growth strategy for the turnaround, specifically as it related to talent. The CEO had a strong technology background and was well-suited to come in and get this organization focused and turned around. He put in place a three-phase plan to be carried out over a six-year period beginning with Phase 1: Get Fit, Phase 2: Win More, and Phase 3: Lead.

Phase 1: _Get Fit – Stabilize the Business (one year)_

This organization was going through growing pains while moving toward becoming a leader in the market and shifting its culture. (See Table 10.1).

Table 10.1: From…To

From		To
• A holding company		• An operating company
• Internally focused product push		• Externally focused – _"customer mindset"_
• Sales only		• Solutions provider
• Fragmented processes		• Partnership model
• Individual achievement		• Integrated operating practices
• Hierarchical decision making		• Getting things done through others
• Little accountability		• Collaborative decision making
• An environment where we blamed others		• Personal accountability
• Survival culture		• A winning culture

This phase was about doing an initial assessment of the organization and ensuring it had the right talent in the right roles. It was also an opportunity to put in place the core common processes necessary to drive the talent. The objective was to transform the organization into a high-performance company, a clear leader and innovator in its chosen markets. As such, it continued to stay focused on six strategic priorities with the talent process as one of the HR levers to drive the key strategic priority: Revitalize the organization through hiring, people development, and succession planning. Having seen this work before, the CEO understood the complexities of a software business and the importance of a common HR and talent process, especially to support the needs of the board of directors.

They began by implementing a common HR system, followed by a common payroll and performance and talent management process. The performance management process included four key steps throughout the year:

- Initial objective-setting and development-planning
- Mid-year review of performance and development
- Informal discussion of performance and development at the third quarter
- End-of-year review of performance and development

They also stressed ongoing business unit reviews and sourcing candidates when needed throughout the year. They created a set of leadership competencies that were related to where it was headed and the kind of leaders it would need to drive the strategy forward; some of these leadership capabilities included cooperative collaboration, strategic agility, leading with integrity, etc. The company began the talent and succession process by engaging the senior leadership and Board in a rigorous approach to review its talent at the top two layers (CEO +2). This approach included an organizational summary of how the organization was getting stronger and what more it still had to do. They reviewed the organization chart and a 4-box that included a look at results and values (client focus, leadership, excellence, aspiration, and results) as well as the succession charts and individual employee profiles. They continued this approach, which evolved as a key initiative, to ensure they had the right talent and successors at all levels of the organization for now and the future. They used their values as the core focus of key behaviors and highlighted expectations for "leader behaviors" that were reinforced in the talent-planning process. Once they were able to stabilize and review the talent, it became clearer where they needed to focus in order to grow their talent.

**Phase 2**: Win More – Platform for Growth (three years)

The focus here was to grow in the marketplace and explore additional opportunities to expand the business. This was a difficult time for the business as the external landscape was changing: financial markets were compromised and there was less money being spent on technology solutions. Additionally, the company needed to focus in the Asia Pacific region and continue to reach deeper into local markets with the help of partners in the technology space. So they embarked on a large acquisition of a different industry outside of the financial space and put a strategy in place to grow through partnership relationships. They became more laser-focused to drive the talent mission: To improve business results and gain competitive advantage now and for the future by identifying and building talent across the organization.

The primary focus of their talent strategy was to identify, develop, and select individuals for critical positions (CEO+2). This process guided their line managers in focusing on sourcing candidates either from within (preferably) or outside of the organization. While this process was intended to identify future leaders, it was neither a guarantee nor a commitment to any individual for a particular future assignment or additional growth. This process also assisted line management in identifying the appropriate developmental experiences necessary to build an individual's leadership skills and thereby maximize their potential. The organization put in place a key manager program in addition to highlighting specific experiences available to support the growth and development of the talent. The organization launched an Essential Manager Program for all managers that focused on the basics. It was important to ensure that the program was delivered in all of the key markets, especially Asia. Consistent training had not existed in the past, so basic coaching and feedback skills were introduced. Senior leaders participated as teachers in these programs. As part of the overall development process, top talent was tapped to lead projects. This approach helped to build common language, models, and behavioral descriptions that helped in the discussion of talent capability.

__Phase 3__: Lead in Our Markets (two years)

As the organization entered the leadership phase of the turnaround, it invested in products/solutions/services. Now it was time to build the organizational capability and leaders to win in the marketplace.

Up until this point, the organization had put in place consistent and repeatable processes that integrated key HR strategies to attract, develop, motivate, and transition employees throughout their careers. An integrated talent management approach was leveraged to provide significant opportunities for interactions among top management, the board, varying business units, key line managers, and HR. The steps were very clear – the CEO management team met face-to-face yearly to review the talent. Business unit leaders were expected to have a six-month follow-up to the CEO management team to report on progress; they also made it a point to include a talent review agenda item at their monthly operations meetings. This helped prepare the CEO for presenting to the yearly report to the board of directors on key talent across the business. The board spent a lot of time at this meeting reviewing the details of the talent presented. They were most interested in the succession plans of the CEO's direct reports and wanted to see progress year after year as they got to know the talent more. Additional opportunities were built in for the board to get to know key leaders by having them present on various occasions. Opportunities were also created for "meet and greets" prior to the board meetings. There were biannual nominations to the senior leadership team (top 50) based on business commitment, performance, demonstration of company values, and leadership. Also in place was a Leadership Excellence Program for the senior leadership team as well as high potentials, high performers, and successors to the top 50. The CEO sponsored the program, so he was available to kick-off each session; members of the team were also available for "fireside chats" at each session. A Leadership Excellence Program was conducted in Asia to demonstrate the company's commitment to growth. The CEO also pulled the top 50 together once a year to collectively set the strategy and put execution plans in place, which they were expected to take back to their teams for implementation.

Ultimately, all of the leaders and managers needed to take clear accountability for ensuring that the growth of their talent was commensurate with their business strategies and aspirations of sustained market growth. This was the final push in becoming leaders in the market and they continued to drive their growth strategy. In addition to the talent actions, they reorganized themselves for success by creating a new regional model and had an increased focus on their partnership model to grow their business. They were well-positioned for an acquisition or another merger.

Most recently, the organization was sold, the CEO left, and there was a change in the entire management team. It took a little over four years to build this talent system, so the question becomes, how is it sustainable? This is a very good question, and as the new HR leader comes in, this person should be thinking about the questions in Exercise 10.2.

Exercise 10.2: Making the Talent System Sustainable

1. What is working well that we need to keep?

_____

_____

_____

2. *What parts of the Talent Optimization Framework™ are missing that will have to be designed in?*

_____

_____

_____

3. *How should we measure success?*

_____

_____

_____

4. *What types of data should be collected to demonstrate success?*

_____

_____

_____

5. *What types of analysis should be completed to gain insight into the talent capability improvement?*

_____

_____

_____

Summary

Contact us at www.lindasharkey.com to discuss your analysis and what you would do next in each of these cases.

_____

CHAPTER ELEVEN

THE LAST WORD
RESULTS AND CONCLUSIONS

Now that you have worked through the components of the Talent Optimization Framework™, you should have a good understanding of your plan and the business impact it will have. Implementation should go smoothly if you pay attention to detail and follow-up. A plan is only as good as its execution. So, know that things can change during implementation, and when they do, you will need to adjust and adapt to the environment and circumstances.

Data-driven decision-making about talent and using scientific methods to quantify human behavior are essential ingredients to creating and executing a top-notch talent plan. These elements add precision, science, predictability, and rigor to the talent management process. If talent management planning is done well, you will be able to use the information to predict:

- Hiring profiles

- Factors that make your company unique

- How to market to those unique factors to attract the right talent

- Flight risk and retention patterns

- Who will make the best leaders

- How to best combine talent capabilities to drive business results

The purpose of the Talent Optimization Framework is to help you take your talent practices to a level of sophistication that predicts and ensures that you have the best talent in the right roles today and in the future. If you use the model correctly, you will know ahead of time when the business environment is changing. Early warning indicators built into the model may signal radical adjustments if market trends shift dramatically. Watch it carefully and the model will help you predict changes so that you can flex ahead of the curve, thus navigating today's challenging business environment successfully.

Now that you have completed the chapters and exercises in this workbook, you have learned a methodology for continuous improvement. The approach will become part of your DNA, not only in how you do business, but also in how you apply science and rigor to your talent development processes.

Making Talent Optimization a Lasting Part of Your Business Equation

The Optimizing Talent approach requires a fair degree of discipline to implement. The framework can be used anywhere in the world in any part of your business and at any level. Using it companywide, all parts of your business will be guided by the same talent principles, and each unit can adapt the principles to their unique business requirements.

The ability to adapt the Optimizing Talent Framework locally is a critical element of this approach. It creates a consistent language for your organization and a rigor that drives complacency out of your human capital approaches. And, it has the added benefit of building in local empowerment. A documented fact in change management theory relative to program implementation is how much personal involvement you and your leadership team have in developing the Optimizing Talent plan whether you are the overall corporate team responsible for the effort, a business unit, or a functional team.

Your ability to tailor the talent plan to your unique needs increases the likelihood of positive implementation exponentially. As cited in the GE Change Acceleration Program; however, your journey does not stop with a one-time interaction of the framework and plan. It must become part of the regular operating rhythm of your business planning and decision-making process to yield lasting and sustainable results. The Talent Optimization plan put forth in this workbook must become part of your culture, i.e. a natural part of how you and your think, to achieve the maximum benefits. When it has become engrained in your leaders relative to how they lead and develop talent, you will be amazed at the results.

Your Talent Brand and Results

After you've had a chance to thoroughly review and implement the information from the preceding chapters, it is time to look at the macro picture. Did your Optimizing Talent plans yield the results you had hoped for? Think about these questions.

- Has your market position improved?

- Is your stock price increasing?

- Are your business results less volatile?

- Has your quality improved?

- Is your customer retention of new and existing customers increasing?

- Are analysts noticing your leadership and talent depth?

- Are you retaining your top talent?

- Have your overall talent recruitment costs gone down?

- Are the best and brightest flocking to your doors at college campuses and recruitment events?

- What marketplace recognition has your company achieved?

Test your brand in the market. Is it reflecting the internal work and value placed on talent? Hold focus groups to measure if your internal brand is seeping into the external market. Check your employee engagement scores and monitor your culture. Are you continually improving and moving toward a high performance culture and increased employee engagement? If so, humbly communicate your message and results, and a critical warning: don't rest on your laurels. Keep using the model, tracking progress, and revising talent plans accordingly. Communicate the results clearly and transparently to everyone in the organization, and most importantly, relay this information to your internal customer. It will reaffirm what they already know firsthand: that your company is a great place for talent!

Roadmap to Success!

As you go on your way, we ask you to remember that you have to do a few things to ensure your greatest success. The list is below, followed by the checklists from each chapter of the book. Photocopy them. Pin them to your office wall. Carry them with you. These are your roadmap to Talent Optimization success!

- Measure progress along the way and at the end of each year.

- Revise your plans accordingly.

- Create an operating rhythm around talent assessment and plans and make it part of your business planning process. Discuss these plans at least quarterly in conjunction with the business plans and results.

- Review your operating hypotheses (discussed in Chapters Three and Four) to see if they hold true or need to be adjusted.

- Use your data to inform and define predictive analytics about your people and culture.

- Apply the predictive analytics to and embed them in your Talent Optimization plan.

- Keep the results in the open. Share feedback on assessments with those assessed. Be transparent in all your talent transactions. Never employ the "black box" approach of keeping talent information in the hands of only a chosen few. It will catch up with you.

- Communicate about your progress and the areas still needing improvement. Be honest and steer clear of marketing "pitches" that skew reality.

Chapter Two Checklist

☐ Do you clearly understand your current talent brand?

- Have you checked social media platforms, jobsites, and employee blog sites?

- Have you researched what people are saying to each other about your organization, your leaders, your organization's career development opportunities?

- Have you reviewed your employee surveys?

☐ What is your employee brand?

- What are you promising new hires?

- What is your employee development plan?

- Are your organization's culture, behaviors, and values aligned? Are these reflected in your employee brand?

☐ What methods/tools do you have in place or could you put in place to measure and improve employee engagement/satisfaction?

- Do you have an employee satisfaction survey?

- Are your leaders coaches/mentors to your employees?

Chapter Three Checklist

☐ Ensure you understand and are able to articulate the alignment between what you do (accountabilities/goals) and why you do it (mission/strategies).

☐ Verify alignment between the goals, the values, and leadership behaviors.

☐ Create a Stop/Start/Keep action plan that drives behaviors which support the values and create the experiences that develop the culture you desire.

☐ Embed these actions into leaders' goals and measures.

☐ Verify that you are developing a talent-supportive culture.

Chapter Four Checklist

☐ Are you clear on the most critical behaviors necessary to drive business outcomes?

☐ Are these behaviors derived from key business imperatives (goals, strategy, vision, mission, values, etc.)?

☐ Have you defined these behaviors in simple terms that everyone can understand and with which everyone can identify?

☐ Do you have key stakeholder buy-in and sign-off?

☐ Do you have a document that is available to use to assess and develop talent in the rest of the Talent Optimization Framework™?

☐ Do you have a communication plan for engaging the rest of the workforce?

Chapter Five Checklist:

☐ Do you have a clear plan for assessing your talent?

☐ Are you clear on the specific areas – skills and behaviors—against which you need to assess talent?

☐ Do you have a systematic process and tools in place for consistent assessment?

☐ Have you articulated what "best" looks like for the organization as well as "good" and "poor," and have you spelled this out in clear and observable terms?

☐ Do you have trained internal human resources talent to conduct an unbiased assessment?

☐ Can you aggregate the assessment data to provide a compelling and actionable picture for the organization to use as the basis for improvement plans?

Chapter Six Checklist

☐ Are you clear on the goals for your current performance management system?

☐ Have you developed specific goals for your new performance management system?

☐ Have you reviewed your current system for brain friendly approaches?

☐ Are the behaviors that are expected in your organization spelled out clearly and are they included in your feedback and review process?

☐ Are your leaders in support of the process, and do they understand their role in ensuring it is effective?

☐ Have your leaders been trained in coaching and brain based feedback?

☐ Do you have methods for training your employees in receiving coaching and feedback?

☐ Do you have a method for measuring the impact of your performance evaluation process?

Chapter Seven Checklist

☐ Are your training strategies aligned to measurable and specific gaps or key future development needs required by the strategic direction of the company?

☐ Has a thorough individual assessment been done?

☐ Is a clear personal action plan in place that can be measured?

☐ Is there a mechanism for follow-up at specified intervals?

☐ Is the follow-up approach systematic and both quantitative and qualitative (bullet points of anecdotal information on improvement is not enough to show impact!)?

☐ Do your learning and development roadmaps employ a wide variety of approaches and more than just classroom based?

Chapter Eight Checklist

☐ Have you assessed yourself relative to the above questions?

☐ Have you assessed your team for its capabilities?

☐ Have you validated you assessment of yourself and your team with other key stakeholders in the organization?

☐ Do you have an honest picture of your team's capability that you can take action on?

☐ Have you shared the results with your team, including your personal results?

☐ Have you created clear development goals for the team?

☐ Do you have a specific action plan in place to close any gaps?

☐ Have you defined how you will measure and track progress?

Chapter Nine Checklist

☐ Do you have a clear hypothesis that everyone can understand?

- Have you tested it with others?

- Is it important to the leadership?

- Is it rooted in the business strategy?

☐ Do you know what data you have relative to the question at hand?

☐ Have you defined the new data you need to collect?

- Have you done an environmental scan to see what data are out there that can inform your question?

- Have you done some scenario planning to clarify possibilities and help you define the variables that will be important to your question or hypothesis?

☐ Did you define a data collection methodology?

- Do you know what business issues you may want to be correlating your data with?

☐ Did you get sign-off on your plan from your key stakeholders?

Parting Thoughts

Finally, let us know your stories. Keep us posted on your progress. Jump onto our website (www. lindasharkey.com) and let us know how you are doing. Tell us what worked what didn't and the best practices you uncovered. Be sure to connect with our "pracademics" for advice and feedback. Just send us a note through our website, and we will get back to you. We're on this journey with you!

Contributing Experts

Phil Dixon is founder of the University of the Brain, an organization that is applying the latest knowledge from the field of integrative neuroscience to the areas of leadership development and organizational & cultural change. He is a frequent speaker on the topic of brain-based leadership and is in the process of writing a new book, *Using Your Brain for a Change*.

Eve Emerson is a human resources executive with demonstrated success in executive coaching, leadership, and organizational development in dynamic global environments like IBM and Chase Manhattan Bank.

Lynda Keating is currently the EVP, Leadership and Culture at ACHIEVEBLUE. A human resources executive specializing in organizational development, leadership, and culture and talent strategy, Lynda works with clients worldwide where she is best known for translating strategy into practical and effective people solutions.

Dan Martin is a leading expert in change management and improving organization performance. He has 40 years of industry experience and human resources leadership in companies such as GE. Currently he is working with healthcare organizations to implement strategic organizational change in response to healthcare reform and the 2010 Affordable Care Act.

Sarah McArthur is founder of *sdedit, a writing and editing firm based in San Diego, California. With two decades of experience in the publishing field, Sarah has worked with such influential clients as Marshall Goldsmith and Anthony Robbins. Sarah is co-editor of the leadership classic *Coaching for Leadership* as well as the Choice Award Winner *The AMA Handbook of Leadership*.

Linda D. Sharkey PhD is a human resources business strategist who specializes in global leadership development and culture transformation. She is an internationally recognized author, speaker and executive coach. Dr. Sharkey is a partner at ACHIEVEBLUE, a boutique leadership development consulting firm and founding member of the Marshall Goldsmith Group.

Liza Sichon is an executive coach, speaker, and human resources consultant with extensive global experience in large corporations. She partners with clients to enable them to achieve financial success, advance their careers, and live fulfilling lives.

Frank Wagner combines designing/facilitating leadership training and one-on-one leadership coaching in a practice that spans more than 30 years. He is known for his common- sense approach, which helps leaders achieve positive, enduring improvement.

Appendix

Exhibit 5.1: Sample Assessment Interview

Look for the following

INTELLIGENCE AND ABILITY
- *Intelligence, cognitive ability*
- *Knowledge*
- *Project results*
- *Communication skills*
- *Judgment, decisiveness*
- *Decision making approach*
- *Academic scores*
- *Career actions*

PERSONALITY
- *Optimism*
- *Self-confidence*
- *Honesty and integrity*
- *Enthusiasm*
- *Charisma*
- *Desire to lead*
- *Independence*

SOCIAL CHARACTERISTICS
- *Sociability, interpersonal skills*
- *Cooperativeness*
- *Ability to enlist cooperation*
- *Tact, diplomacy*

EMOTIONAL INTELLIGENCE
- *Self-awareness, self-assessment*
- *Self-esteem*
- *Motivation*
- *Empathy*
- *Optimism, realism*

WORK-RELATED CHARACTERISTICS
- *Experience (jobs held, markets, industries, managerial)*
- *Personal drive, desire to excel*
- *Results achieved (specific accomplishments, track record)*
- *Responsibility in pursuit of goals*
- *Persistence against obstacles, tenacity*
- *Education, social background*
- *Communication, coaching*
- *Mobility*

PERSONAL CHARACTERISTICS
- *Authenticity*
- *Energy*
- *Passion*
- *Physical stamina*

Beginning

In our organization, we believe that the more we know about the individual, the better we can help him or her develop and meet his or her goals. I'd like to learn all about your work experience your education and training, your strengths and development areas, your goals, and your outside interests.

Create a relaxed environment	*Ask open-ended questions*
Avoid interruptions – have privacy	*Topic agenda items with breaks*
Make introductions first	*Stress importance of openness*
Introduce, note take and role	*Answer questions he/she may have*
Start with small talk	*Be supportive*

Education and Training

Let's talk about your education starting with the level just below college/university and working up to today. This includes college/university, graduate school, company training, and any external courses. I'd like to know about the subjects you like and dislike and why, special academic achievements, extra-curricular activities, and your results (i.e. grade point average).

Best and worst subjects (why)	*Quantifiable measurements, GPA*
Extracurricular activities	*Leadership roles*
Reason for selecting school(s)	*Reason for selecting major or courses*
Honors, other recognition	*Relation to career*
Skills required	*Transition-high school to college*

Work History/Experience

Let's begin by looking at your work experience. Tell me about your previous jobs, starting from the first one up to today. I'd like to hear how you were hired for each job. Then give me a description of each job. Tell me about your responsibilities and accomplishments, what you liked and disliked about the job and what you learned about yourself as a result of the experience.

How did you get the job?	*Scope of impact and responsibilities*
Significant accomplishments (quantify)	*Likes and dislikes*
Skills required	*Global experience*
Leadership /team experience	*Why did you leave the job?*
Frustrations	*Initiative/innovativeness*
Supervision/independence	*Supervisor's style – likes/dislikes*
Learnings along the way	

Self-assessment of Strengths and Development Areas

Strengths	What have you learned about yourself and your personal strengths through your work and educational experiences? For example, do you have better interpersonal skills than most, or better organization skills, or better analytical skills?
Development areas	What have you learned about yourself and your development needs through your work and education experiences? We all have areas we could improve and recognizing your own development needs a big step toward improvement. For example, do you pay too much attention to details or do you lack coaching skills?

Five to six strengths

Two to three development areas in detail

What training can address the needs?

Plans and Goals for the Future

Where do you see career heading? Where do you want to go next? Where do you see yourself in five to ten years?

Line vs. staff interests   *Global interests*

Industry preferences   *Market preferences*

Steps needed to reach career goals   *Location preferences*

Job Satisfaction

What gives you real job satisfaction? Motivations differ from person to person. For example, some people seek money while others seek job security. Some want to manage while others want to be expert independent contributors. Some want to be creative, while others seek structure. What do you like in a job?

Ambitions Independent/Dependent

Structured/unstructured   *Unknown/known*

How does pressure affect you?   *What is the most important criticism you received from a senior manager?*

Outside Interests

Tell me about your hobbies and other interests. Do you do any community activities? How seriously do you peruse these interests?

Closing

Thank you for your candor. We have a great picture of your background and goals. Is there anything else you would like to bring up?

Wish the candidate all the best with his or her career and explain the next steps.

Additional Questions

- In your last three jobs, what were your most significant accomplishments?
- In the past 12 months, what were your toughest decisions and why?
- What would your peers, subordinates, and managers say about you?
- What were the biggest mistakes you made in the last couple of years? Why?
- What one or two things could you do better to be a better leader?
- What two people, events, or circumstances shaped you?

Reference Checking Model

Before the calls

- Complete preliminary assessee's strength and development areas
- Identify themes or patterns of interest and issues to probe
- Review list of reference questions for applicability and select appropriate questions
- Set up mutually convenient date/time for discussion

During the call

- Identify yourself and your role, establish a rapport
- Explain the process and its importance
- Confirm assessee's permission and mutual expectation – in unlikely event an individual is not comfortable providing a reference, probe as to why not?
- Establish confidentiality
- Reconfirm time will allow for about 45 minutes conversion

Reference Checking Questions

- Could you briefly describe the nature of the relationship with (assessee)?

How have you worked together? What was the length of the association?

- What do you see as (assessee's) strengths/attributes? Provide examples.

- If you could make two or three suggestions to increase higher impact/effectiveness, what would they be?

- How would you characterize (assessee's) leadership style? How have you seen the leadership traits demonstrated?

- How does his/her style change under pressure?

- In your experience, how would you describe him/her as a team member? Coach?

- How does (assessee) influence others around him/her?

- How would you describe (assessee's) communication style? Suggestions for improvement? Is there an area where (assessee) excels or particularly differentiates himself/herself form others you have worked with?

- How is (assessee) regarded in your business? What is he/she known for? Reputation?

- Have you ever provided feedback to him/her before? If so, how have you seen him or her change? Questions specific to interview learnings. (Example: Others have characterized (assessee) as being (e.g. aggressive) would you agree with this or not and why?

- Questions to human resource managers only: What type of next role would make sense for (assessee)? What type of business setting would he/she do best? What would you like to see (assessee) demonstrate to warrant further advancement in his/her career?

- Anything we have not touched on?

Reference Checking Model

During the call wrap up

- Thank the individual for taking the time to provide a reference and for participating in our Optimizing Talent Program

- Provide your contact information should the reference think of additional information to add

After the call

- Summarize your notes to ensure completeness

- Start to identify and synthesize key themes throughout all reference checks

- Incorporate information from reference checks in formal report, as applicable

Exercise 6.1: HR Review

Check the box if your answer is yes.

The organizational context

☐ My organization has a high-trust, low-political environment.

☐ Our company culture is commensurate with growth and candid feedback.

☐ The leaders of our organization are role models for taking performance feedback and changing.

The performance review system itself

☐ The performance review system is clearly separated from the compensation, remuneration, and bonus systems.

☐ The purpose of the performance review system is clear to all.

☐ The performance review system operates efficiently and effectively.

☐ The performance review system is not time-consuming.

☐ The performance review system encourages ongoing feedback and coaching.

☐ The periodic performance reviews are simply reviews of data that have already been discussed.

☐ The performance review system exists in tandem with world-class leadership training for managers and leaders.

The performance review environment

☐ The current organizational context is relatively stable.

☐ Recent changes have been seen as positive.

☐ The company is performing well.

☐ Recent re-organizations, promotions, etc., have been seen as positive.

☐ There is a defined coaching model that managers have been trained on and use.

☐ All HR and company systems align with and support the performance review system

☐ The keepers and monitors of the performance system are trusted.

The manager

☐ Managers have been trained in the need to have regular, ongoing performance conversations.

☐ Regular performance conversations occur most of the time.

☐ Performance conversations are linked to managers' reviews and bonuses.

☐ In most cases, there is a trusted and credible relationship between the manager and the subordinates.

☐ In general, our managers are unbiased (i.e., fair and objective) in their reviews of performance.

☐ Our managers are generally well-informed regarding the performance of their subordinates.

☐ Our managers usually seek out opinions from others about their subordinates.

☐ In general, our managers have the courage to present their own opinions.

☐ In general, our managers understand the aspirations, goals, and makeup of their subordinates.

☐ Our managers have been trained on how to coach and have career conversations.

☐ Managers are coached to alter the timing and delivery of the performance review process in order to be sensitive to what else is going on in the social and work life of the subordinate.

☐ Managers always take enough preparation time for the performance review process for each of their subordinates.

The performance review form

☐ Our performance review form is always completed by the subordinate before the manager.

☐ Our performance review form is brief and to the point.

☐ Our performance review form is easy to understand.

☐ Our performance review form reflects a developmental focus.

☐ Our performance review form includes an area that focuses on career goals.

☐ Our performance review form includes an area that captures ONE short-term career step.

☐ Our performance review form has an area for the identification of three to five strengths.

☐ Our performance review form includes an area that captures ONE short-term developmental area.

☐ Our performance review form has an area that encourages a discussion that links the subordinate's strengths to a particular development area.

☐ Our performance review form has an area to link developmental area to the short-term career goal step.

The performance review event

☐ The subordinate is always involved in setting the time and place of the performance review discussion.

☐ The performance review discussion always take place in private and on "neutral" ground – not the manager's office.

☐ The performance review discussion always takes place in two parts, separated by a reasonable period of time.

The subordinate

☐ Everyone in the company who receives feedback has been trained or given coaching on how to receive feedback.

☐ Everyone in the company who receives feedback has been trained or given coaching on how to change as a result of feedback.

☐ Subordinates have been trained on how to recognize whether they have a fixed or growth mind-set, and how this impacts their receptivity to feedback and the likelihood of a subsequent change.

☐ The subordinate has demonstrated learning and change in the past.

The feedback content

☐ When narrative comments are included, they are clear, focused, and actionable.

☐ Narrative comments are always limited in number.

☐ The performance review content is always structured in a way that encourages discussion and
☐ enquiry rather than simply presenting ratings, numbers, or grades.

☐ The performance review content always leads to a discussion about a single goal.

☐ If there is a need to address the "self" conundrums outlined above – i.e., if there are "self" or behavioral issues--then the manager has made extra effort to be doubly clear on the best manner to get those across.

☐ If the feedback is about "self," the manager always ensures that the ability or behavior described relates to a task or goal that is important to the subordinate.

☐ All content feedback is linked to the performance of the subordinate against a predetermined profile or set of goals.

☐ All content aligns with the recipient's sense of self or desired future.

Follow-up

☐ Managers always follow up with the subordinate at periodic intervals to review and coach progress against the subordinate's goal.

☐ Managers are able to get third-party assistance if required for the subordinate to achieve the goal that has been set.

Brain-friendly process

☐ Managers understand the basics of how the brain works.

☐ Managers have been trained on the impact of various actions on the brain.

☐ Managers understand the impact of their own non-conscious biases, patterns, and triggers.

☐ Subordinates have adequate input into the process and content of the performance review.

☐ All communications and written documentation are constructed with the brain in mind.

☐ The systems and processes are seen as fair.

Exercise 6.2: Managers' and Leaders' Review

Note that not all components are relevant to the individual manager or leader, as they may be outside his/or scope and/or authority. Check the box if your answer is yes.

The departmental context

☐ You have created a high-trust, low-political environment in your department.

☐ You have created a culture in your department that is commensurate with growth and candid feedback.

☐ You are a role model for taking performance feedback and changing appropriately.

The performance review system

☐ You clearly separate the performance review system from the compensation, remuneration, and bonus systems (Note: as manager, you may not have the authority to do this).

☐ You are clear as to the purpose of the performance review system, and you have made it clear to the people who work for you.

☐ You operate the performance review system as efficiently and effectively as possible.

☐ You operate the performance review system in the least time-consuming fashion possible.

☐ You use the performance review system as a part of ongoing feedback process.

☐ The performance review is simply a review of data that you have already discussed with the people who work for you.

☐ You have received world-class training in all aspects that relate to performance reviews.

The performance review environment

☐ Your current departmental context is relatively stable.

☐ Any recent changes that you have made to the department have been seen as positive.

☐ Your department is performing well.

☐ Any recent re-organizations, promotions, etc., that you have made to the department have been seen as positive.

☐ You have been trained on and are adept at using a defined coaching model.

☐ You believe that all of the HR and company systems align with and support the performance review system.

☐ You trust the keepers and monitors of the performance system.

You – yes, you – the manager!

☐ You have been trained in the need to have regular ongoing performance conversations.

☐ You hold regular performance conversations.

☐ Your review and bonus are linked to the fact that you hold performance conversations.

☐ You have been trained in how to have performance improvement conversations.

☐ You have a trusted and credible relationship with the people who work for you, or are willing to do what it takes to develop that sense of trust and credibility if it is not in place.

☐ You are unbiased (i.e., fair and objective) in your reviews.

☐ You are well informed regarding the performance of the people who work for you.

☐ You seek out opinions from others about the people who work for you.

☐ You have the courage to present your own opinions and not hide behind the opinions of others.

☐ You understand the aspirations, goals, and makeup of the people who work for you.

☐ You have been trained in how people respond to feedback, and how they change as a result.

☐ You have been trained how to coach.

☐ You have been trained how to have career conversations.

☐ You understand the positivity and negativity biases of the people who work for you.

☐ You have been coached to alter the timing and delivery of the performance review process in order to be sensitive to what else is going on in the social and work lives of the people who work for you

☐ You understand whether the subordinate has a fixed ("I know") or a growth ("I can learn") mindset.

☐ You always take enough preparation time for the performance review process for each of your subordinates.

The performance review form

☐ The people who work for you complete the performance review form before you make your comments.

☐ You only use those parts of the performance review form that are brief and to the point.

☐ You and your subordinates all fully understand the performance review form.

☐ You utilize the performance review form as a basis to reflect a developmental focus in your discussions with the people who work for you.

☐ You include a focus on career goals in your performance review discussions.

☐ You always ensure that ONE short-term career step is captured on the performance review form.

☐ You always ensure that three to five strengths are captured on the performance review form and that these strengths are acknowledged and talked about in your discussions with the people who work for you.

☐ You always ensure that ONE, and only ONE, short-term developmental area is captured on the performance review form.

☐ You always discuss how the strengths of the person who works for you are linked to their development area.

☐ You always discuss how the development area of the person who works for you is linked to their short-term career goal step.

The performance review event

☐ The people who work for you are always involved in setting the time and place of their performance review discussion.

☐ The performance review discussions always take place in private and on "neutral" ground – not in your office.

☐ You always hold the performance review discussion in two parts, separated by a reasonable period of time.

The subordinate

☐ The people who work for you have been trained or given coaching on receiving feedback.

☐ The people who work for you have been trained or given coaching on changing after having received feedback.

☐ You alter the timing and delivery of the performance review process in order to be sensitive to what else is going on in the social and work life of the people who work for you.

☐ The people who work for you have been trained to understand their own positivity and negativity biases and how these impact their receptivity to feedback and the likelihood of their making a subsequent change.

☐ The people who work for you have been trained on how to recognize whether they have a fixed or growth mind-set, and how this impacts their receptivity to feedback and the likelihood of a subsequent change.

☐ The people who work for you have been able to demonstrate learning and change in the past.

The feedback content

☐ Any narrative comments you have included are clear, focused, and actionable.

☐ You always limit the number of narrative comments you make.

☐ You always structure the performance review conversation in a way that encourages discussion, conversation, and enquiry rather than simply presenting ratings, numbers, or grades.

☐ You always translate the performance review content into a discussion about a single goal.

☐ If your feedback includes aspects of "self" or behavioral issues, then you have taken extra effort to be doubly clear on the best manner to get those across. You always take guidance from HR.

☐ If your feedback includes aspects of "self" or behavioral issues, then you are able to relate these to a task or goal that is important to your subordinate.

☐ You always review the performance of the person who works for you against a pre-determined profile or set of goals.

☐ The feedback that you are giving to the person who works for you aligns with that person's sense of self or desired future.

Follow-up

☐ You always follow up with the people who work for you at periodic intervals to review and coach their progress against their goals.

☐ You are able to get third-party assistance for your subordinates if it is required for them to achieve the goal that has been set for them.

Brain-friendly process

☐ Do you understand the basics of how the brain works?

☐ Have you been trained on the impact of your actions and statements on the brain of the people who work for you?

☐ Do you understand the impact of your own non-conscious biases, patterns, and triggers?

☐ Do you engage the people who work for you in the process and content of their performance review?

☐ Do you communicate and document your conversations with the brain in mind?

☐ Do all of the people who work for you see your actions and communications as fair? This includes your day-to-day interactions with them, as well as those actions which are part of the performance review.

☐ Do you know how the people who work for you rank the various brain threats that can occur?

References

Bersin, J. (2013, May 6). Time to scrap performance appraisals? *Forbes*. Retrieved October 3, 2013 from *forbes.com/sites/joshbersin/2013/05/06/time-to-scrap-performance-appraisals*.

Bersin, J., O'Lard, K., and Audia, W. W. (2013, September). High-impact talent analytics: building a world-class HR measurement and analytics function. (*bersin.com/library*)

Bracken, D. W., Timmreck, C. W., and Church, A.H. (2001). *The Handbook of Multisource Feedback*. San Francisco, CA: Jossey-Bass.

Coens, T. and Jenkins, M. (2002). *Abolishing Performance Appraisals: Why They Backfire and What To Do Instead*. San Francisco, CA: Berrett-Kohler.

Conaty, B. and Charan, R. (2010). *The Talent Masters: Why Smart Leaders Put People Before Numbers*. New York: Crown Publishing Group.

D'Aprix, R. (1996). *Communicating for Change: Connecting the Workplace With the Marketplace*. San Francisco, CA: Jossey-Bass.

Deming, W. E. (1982). *Out of Crisis*. Cambridge, MA: MIT Press

DeNisi, A. and Kluger, A. N. (2000). *Feedback Effectiveness: Can 360-degree Appraisals Be Improved?* Academy of Management Executive,14(1), 129-138.

Dixon, H.P. and Underwood, W. (2010). Unpublished research for Silicon Valley Hi-Tech company.

Drucker, P. F. (2001). *The Essential Drucker*. New York: HarperBusiness.

Fear, R. and Chiron, R. (2002). *The Evaluation Interview: How to Probe Deeply, Get Candid Answers, and Predict the Performance of Job Candidates* (5th ed.). New York: McGraw Hill.

Ferstl, K. L. and Bruskiewicz, K. T. (2000, April). Self-other Agreement and Cognitive Reactions to Multirater Feedback. Paper presented at the 15th Annual Conference of the Society of Industrial and Organizational Psychology (SIOP), New Orleans, LA.

Hogan, J., Hogan, R., and Kaiser, R. B. (2010). Management Derailment: Personality Assessment and Mitigation. In S. Zedeck (Ed.), *APA Handbook of Industrial and Organizational Psychology.* Washington, D.C.: American Psychological Association.

Goldsmith, M. (2002, summer). Try Feedforward Instead of Feedback. *Leader to Leader.*

Goldsmith, M. (2010). *Mojo: How to Get It, How to Keep It, and How to Get It Back If You Lose It.* New York: Hyperion.

Gordon, E. (2012). *Brain Revolution: Train Your Brain to Freedom.* San Francisco, CA: Brain Revolution Publications.

Kluger, A. N. & DeNisi, A. (1996). The effects of feedback interventions on performance: a historical review, a meta-analysis, and a preliminary feedback intervention theory. *Psychological Bulletin,* 119, 2, 254-284.

Lombardo, M. & Eichinger, R. (2004). *FYI: For Your Improvement.* Minneapolis, MN: Lominger Ltd., Inc.

Schein, E. (2004). *Organizational Culture and Leadership* (3rd ed.). San Francisco, CA: Jossey-Bass.

Sharkey, L. D. & Eccher, P. H. (2010). *Optimizing Talent: What Every Leader and Manager Needs to Know to Sustain the Ultimate Workforce.* Charlotte, NC: Information Age Publishing.

Smart, B. D. 2012. *Topgrading: The Proven Hiring and Promoting Method that Turbocharges Company Performance* (3rd ed.). New York: Penguin Group.

Smither, J. W. & Walker, A. G. (2004). Are the characteristics of narrative comments related to improvement in multirater feedback ratings over time? *Journal of Applied Psychology,* 89, 3, 575-581.

Szumal, J. (2002). An international study of the reliability and validity of leadership/impact (L/I)TM. San Francisco, CA: Human Synergistics/Center for Applied Research.